THE

EMANCIPATION

OF WOMEN

From the Writings of
V. I. LENIN

Preface by NADEZHDA K. KRUPSKAYA

*With an Appendix, "Lenin on the
Woman Question" by* CLARA ZETKIN

INTERNATIONAL PUBLISHERS
New York

The writings included in this volume are from works previously issued by
International Publishers: V. I. Lenin, *Women and Society* (1938); Karl Marx,
Frederick Engels, V. I. Lenin and Joseph Stalin, *The Woman Question* (1951);
and Clara Zetkin, *Reminiscences of Lenin* (1934); as well as from V. I. Lenin,
Collected Works, © by Lawrence & Wishart, London, 1963-69.

NOTE ON REFERENCES: Asteriks refer to footnotes on page, superior numbers
to Notes, pp. 124-131.

SBN 7178-0290-6

Printed in the United States of America

Contents

In the course of his revolutionary activities Lenin often wrote and spoke about the emancipation of working women in general and peasant women in particular. To be sure, the emancipation of women is inseparably bound up with the entire struggle for the workers' cause, for socialism. We know Lenin as the leader of the working people, as the organiser of the Party and Soviet government, as a fighter and builder. Every working woman, every peasant woman must know about all that Lenin did, every aspect of his work, without limiting herself to what Lenin said about the position of working women and their emancipation. But because there exists the closest connection between the entire struggle of the working class and improving the position of women, Lenin often—on more than forty occasions, in fact—referred to this question in his speeches and articles, and every one of these references was inseparably bound up with all the other things that were of interest and concern to him at the time.

From the very start of his revolutionary career Comrade Lenin paid special attention to the position of women workers and peasants and to drawing them into the working-class movement. Lenin did his first practical revolutionary work in St. Petersburg (now Leningrad), where he organised a group of Social-Democrats which became extremely active among the St. Petersburg workers, publishing illegal leaflets and distributing them at factories. The leaflets were usually addressed to the workmen. At that time the class consciousness of the mass of the workers was still little developed, the most backward among them being working women.

They received very low wages and their rights were flagrantly violated. So the leaflets were usually addressed to the men (the two leaflets addressed to the working women of the Laferm tobacco factory were an exception). Lenin also wrote a leaflet for the workers of the Tornton cloth mill (in 1895) and although the women working there were most backward, he entitled the leaflet: "To the Working Men and Women of the Tornton Mill." This is a detail, but a very important one.

When he was in exile in 1899, Lenin corresponded with the Party organisation (the First Party Congress was held in 1898) and mentioned the subjects he wanted to write about in the illegal press. These included a pamphlet called "Women and the Workers' Cause". In this pamphlet Lenin intended to describe the position of women factory workers and peasant women and to show that the only salvation for them was through their participation in the revolutionary movement, and that only the victory of the working class would bring emancipation to women workers and peasants.

Writing in 1901 about the women who took part in the Obukhov defence,[1] about the speech delivered by a woman worker Marfa Yakovleva in court, Lenin said:

"The memory of our heroic comrades murdered and tortured to death in prison will increase tenfold the strength of the new fighters and will rouse thousands to rally to their aid, and like the eighteen-year-old Marfa Yakovleva, they will openly say: 'We stand by our brothers!' In addition to reprisals by the police and the military against participants in demonstrations, the government intends to prosecute them for rebellion; we will retaliate by uniting our revolutionary forces and winning over to our side all who are oppressed by the tyranny of tsarism, and by systematically preparing for the uprising of the whole people!"*

Lenin made a close study of the life and labour conditions of women factory workers, peasants and women employed in the handicrafts.

While in prison, Lenin studied the position of peasants as revealed by statistical reports; he studied the influence of the handicrafts, the drift of the peasants to the factories and the influence exerted by the factories on their culture

---

* V. I. Lenin, *Collected Works,* Vol. 5, pp. 248-49.—*Ed.*

and way of life. At the same time he studied all these questions from the viewpoint of women's labour. He pointed out that the peasant's proprietorial psychology places on women a burden of unnecessary and senseless drudgery (every peasant woman of a large family clearing only the small part of the table she eats on, cooking a separate meal for her own child and milking a cow to get only just enough milk for her own child).

In his book *The Development of Capitalism in Russia* Lenin describes how cattle farmers exploit peasant women, how the merchant-buyers exploit women lace-weavers; he shows that large-scale industry emancipates women and that the work at factories broadens their outlook, makes them more cultured and independent and helps them to break the shackles of patriarchal life. Lenin said that the development of large-scale industry would create the basis for complete emancipation of women. Characteristic in this respect is Lenin's article "A Great Technical Achievement" written in 1913.

Workers in the bourgeois countries must fight for equal rights for men and women.

In exile Lenin devoted much of his time to working out the Party programme. At that time the Party had no programme. There was only a draft programme compiled by the Emancipation of Labour group.[2] Examining this programme in his article "A Draft Programme of Our Party" and commenting on §9 of the practical part of the programme, which demanded "the revision of our entire civil and criminal legislation, the abolition of social-estate divisions and of punishments incompatible with the dignity of man", Lenin wrote that it would be well to add here: "*complete equality of rights for men and women.*"* (My italics—*N. K.*)

In 1903, when the Party Programme was adopted, this clause was included in it.

In 1907, in his report on the International Congress in Stuttgart[3] Lenin noted with satisfaction that the Congress condemned the opportunist practices of the Austrian Social-Democrats who, while conducting a campaign for electoral rights for men, put off the struggle for electoral rights for women to "a later date".

---

* V I. Lenin, *Collected Works*, Vol. 4, p. 239.—*Ed.*

The Soviet government established full equality of rights for men and women.

"We in Russia no longer have the base, mean and infamous denial of rights to women or inequality of the sexes, that disgusting survival of feudalism and medievalism which is being renovated by the avaricious bourgeoisie ... in every other country in the world without exception."*

In 1913, studying the forms of bourgeois democracy and exposing the hypocrisy of the bourgeoisie, Lenin also dealt with the problem of prostitution and showed how, while encouraging white slave traffic and raping girls in the colonies, representatives of the bourgeoisie at the same time hypocritically pretended to be campaigning against prostitution.

Lenin returned to this question in December 1919, when he wrote that "free, civilised" America was touting for women for bawdy houses in the vanquished countries.**

In close connection with this question Lenin examined the question of child-bearing and indignantly wrote of the appeal of some intellectuals to the workers to practise birth control on the grounds that their children were doomed to poverty and privation. This is a petty-bourgeois view, wrote Lenin. The workers take a different view. Children are our future. As for poverty and so on, this can be remedied. We are fighting against capitalism and when we win a victory we shall build a bright future for our children. ...

And finally, in 1916-17, when he could see the socialist revolution was drawing near and was considering what the essential elements of socialist construction would be, and how to draw the masses into this construction, he particularly stressed the need to draw working women into social work, the need to enable all women to work for the benefit of society. *Eight* of his articles written in this period deal with this question, which he links up with the need to organise social life under socialism along new lines. Lenin saw a direct connection between this and the drawing of the most backward groups of women into the work of ruling the country, the need for re-educating the masses in the actual process of social work.

---

* See p. 88 of this book.—*Ed.*
** V. I. Lenin, *Collected Works*, Vol. 30, "Address to the Second All-Russia Congress of Communist Organisations of the Peoples of the East", November 22, 1919.—*Ed.*

Social work teaches the art of government. "We are not utopians," Lenin wrote before the October Revolution. "We know that an unskilled labourer or a cook cannot immediately get on with the job of state administration. In this we agree with the Cadets,[4] with Breshkovskaya, and with Tsereteli. We differ, however, from these citizens in that we demand an immediate break with the prejudiced view that only the rich, or officials chosen from rich families, are capable of *administering* the state, of performing the ordinary, everyday work of administration. We demand that *training* in the work of state administration be conducted by class-conscious workers and soldiers and that this training be begun at once, i.e., that a *beginning* be made at once in training all the working people, all the poor, for this work."*

We know that the Soviet government has done all it can to draw working women in the town and countryside into the work of administration. And we know what great successes have been achieved on this front.

Lenin warmly greeted the awakening of the women of the Soviet East. Since he attached particular importance to raising the level of the nationalities that had been oppressed by tsarism and capitalism, it is quite understandable why he so warmly greeted the conference of delegates of the Women's Departments of Soviet regions and republics in the East.

Speaking of the achievements of the Second Congress of the Communist International, Lenin pointed out that "the Congress will strengthen the ties with the communist movement of women, thanks to the international conference of working women called at the same time."**

In October 1932 we observed the fifteenth anniversary of Soviet power and summed up our achievements on all fronts, including the front of women's emancipation.

We know that women took a very active part in the Civil War, that many of them died in action but many others were steeled in battle. Some women were awarded the Order of the Red Banner for the active part they played in the struggle for Soviets during the Civil War. Many

---

* See p. 55 of this book.—*Ed.*
** V. I. Lenin, *Collected Works*, Vol. 31, "The Second Congress of the Communist International".—*Ed.*

former women partisans now occupy important posts. Women have been persistent in learning to conduct social work.

Delegates' conferences[5] are a school of social work. In 15 years almost 10 million women delegates have passed through this school.

At the time when we observed the fifteenth anniversary of the October Revolution 20 to 25 per cent of the deputies of the village Soviets, district executive committees and city Soviets were women. There were 186 women members oi the All-Russia Central Executive Committee and the Central Executive Committee of the U.S.S.R. On this work they attain ever higher standards.

The number of women members of the Communist Party has also been steadily growing. In 1922 there were only 40,000 but by October 1932 the number exceeded 500,000.

Much progress has been made recently in fulfilling Lenin's behest concerning the complete emancipation of women.

In the last few years large-scale industry has been developing on a tremendous scale. It is being reorganised on the basis of modern technology and scientific organisation of labour. The socialist emulation and shock-workers' movement which have now been widely adopted stimulate a new, communist attitude towards labour. And it must be said that women are not lagging behind men in this. Every day we see more and more front-rank women workers who display great stamina and perseverance in labour. Labour is not something women have to get used to. Under the old regime the lives of women were full of continual, unending labour, but it was the kind of labour that was looked down upon and bore the imprint of bondage. And now this labour training and perseverance in labour place women in the front ranks of the builders of socialism and heroes of labour.

Collectivisation of agriculture was of the utmost importance for the emancipation of women. From the very start Lenin regarded the collectivisation of agriculture as a way of reorganising it along socialist lines. Back in 1894, in his book *What the Friends of the People Are* Lenin quoted Marx's words to the effect that after "the expropriation of the expropriators" is accomplished, that is, when the land-owners are dispossessed of their landed estates and the capitalists of their factories, free workers will be united into co-operatives and the communal ("collective", as Lenin explained) ownership of the land and the means of production they create will be established.

Following the October Revolution, which marked the beginning of "the expropriation of the expropriators", the Soviet government raised the question of organising agricultural artels and communes. Particular attention was paid to this back in 1918 and 1919, but many years passed (as Lenin had predicted) before collectivisation became extensive and struck deep roots. The years of the Civil War, when the class struggle swept the country, the progress of Soviet power in the villages, the help, the cultural assistance rendered by the Soviet government to the countryside—all this prepared the ground for collectivisation, which is developing and growing stronger in the struggle against the kulaks.[6]

Small-scale and middle peasant farming shackled women, tied them to the individual households, and narrowed their outlook; they were in fact slaves of their husbands, who often beat them cruelly. Small-scale farming paved the way for religion. The peasants used to say: "Each man for himself and God for all." Lenin quoted this saying on many occasions, as it perfectly expressed the psychology of a small proprietor. Collectivisation transforms the peasant from a small proprietor into a collectivist, undermines the peasants' isolation and the hold of religion and emancipates women. Lenin said that socialism alone would bring emancipation for women. His words are now coming true. We can see how women's position has changed in the collective farms.

The Congress of front-rank collective farmers held in the middle of February is striking evidence of the headway made in the collective cultivation of the land. There are now 200,000 collective farms, as compared with the 6,000 we had before. The Congress discussed the question of the best way to organise work on the collective farms. There were many women among the delegates. Sopina, a collective farmer from the Central Black Earth Region, made a fine speech which evoked thunderous applause. When she takes a hand in collective-farm development, the peasant woman grows in stature, learns to govern and to fight resolutely against the kulaks, the class enemy. . . .

Religion is losing ground. Now collective-farm women come to the library and say: "You always give me books that simply say that there is no God. I know that without reading books. Give me a book that will tell me how and why religion arose and how and why it will die away." In the last few years there has been a tremendous growth of political consciousness of the masses. Political departments at the machine and tractor stations[7] (whose membership also includes women's organisers) will help not only to consolidate the collective farms, but will also help collective farmers, men and women, to get rid of surviving prejudices and cultural backwardness; lack of rights for women will become a thing of the past.

Ten years have passed since the day of Lenin's death. On that sad day we shall check the fulfilment of all of Lenin's behests. We shall sum up the results. Lenin's behest concerning the emancipation of women is being fulfilled under the guidance of the Party. We shall continue to advance along this path.

November 30, 1933

N. Krupskaya

FROM The Development of Capitalism in Russia

Chapter VI

Capitalist Manufacture and Capitalist Domestic Industry (Abridged)

Further, capitalist domestic industry inevitably entails extremely insanitary working conditions. The utter poverty of the worker, the utter impossibility of controlling working conditions by regulations of any kind, and the combination of the living and working premises, such are the conditions that convert the dwellings of the home workers into hotbeds of infection and occupational disease. In the large establishments one can fight such things; domestic industry, however, is in this respect the most "liberal" form of capitalist exploitation.

An excessively long working day is also an essential feature of domestic work for the capitalist and of the small industries in general. Instances have been given illustrating the comparative length of the working day in the "factories" and among the "handicraftsmen".

The drawing of women and of children of the tenderest age into production is nearly always observed in domestic industry. To illustrate this, let us cite some facts from a description of the women's industries of Moscow Gubernia. There are 10,004 women engaged in cotton winding; children start work at the age of 5 or 6 (!); daily earnings are 10 kopeks, yearly 17 rubles. The working day in the women's industries in general is as much as 18 hours. In the knitting industry children start work from the age of six, daily earnings are 10 kopeks, yearly 22 rubles. Altogether 37,514 females are employed in the women's industries; they begin working from the age of 5 or 6 (in 6 out of 19 industries, which 6 industries account for 32,400 female workers); the average daily earnings are 13 kopeks, yearly 26 rubles 20 kopeks.*

One of the most pernicious aspects of capitalist domestic industry is that it leads to a reduction in the level of the worker's requirements. The employer is able to recruit workers in remote districts where the popular standard of living is particularly low and where the worker's connection with the land enables him to work for a bare pittance. For example, the owner of a village stocking establishment explains that in Moscow rents are high and that, besides, the knitters "have to be ... supplied with white bread, ... whereas here the workers do the job in their own cottages and eat black bread.... Now how can Moscow compete with us!"** In the cotton-winding industry the explanation of the very low wages is that for the peasants' wives, daughters, etc., this is merely a supplementary source of income. "Thus, the system prevailing in this trade forces down to the utmost limit the wages of those for whom it is the sole means of livelihood, reduces the wages of those who obtain their livelihood exclusively by factory labour below their minimum needs, or retards the raising of their standard of living. In both cases it creates extremely abnormal conditions."*** "The factory seeks cheap weavers," says Mr. Kharizomenov, "and it finds them in their native villages, far from the centres of industry.... That wages drop steadily as one moves from the industrial centres to the outer regions is an undoubted fact."**** Hence, the employers are perfectly well able to take advantage of the conditions which artificially tie the population to the rural districts.

---

* Mme. Gorbunova, who has described the women's industries, wrongly gives the earnings as 18 kopeks and 37 rubles 77 kopeks respectively, for she takes only the average figures for each industry and leaves out of account the different numbers of women working in the different industries.
** *Statistical Returns for Moscow Gubernia*, Vol. VII, Pt. II, p. 104.
*** *Statistical Returns for Moscow Gubernia*, Vol. VII, Pt. II, p. 285.
**** *Industries of Vladimir Gubernia*, III, 63. Cf. ibid., 250.

Chapter VII

The Development of Large-Scale Machine Industry (Abridged)

Large-scale machine industry, which concentrates masses of workers who often come from various parts of the country, absolutely refuses to tolerate survivals of patriarchalism and personal dependence, and is marked by a truly "contemptuous attitude to the past". It is this break with obsolete tradition that is one of the substantial conditions which have created the possibility and evoked the necessity of regulating production and of public control over it. In particular, speaking of the transformation brought about by the factory in the conditions of life of the population, it must be stated that the drawing of women and juveniles into production* is, at bottom, progressive. It is indisputable that the capitalist factory places these categories of the working population in particularly hard conditions, and that for them it is particularly necessary to regulate and shorten the working day, to guarantee hygienic conditions of labour, etc.; but endeavours completely to ban the work of women and juveniles in industry, or to maintain the patriarchal manner of life that ruled out such work, would be reactionary and utopian. By destroying the patriarchal isolation of these categories of the population who formerly never emerged from the narrow circle of domestic, family relationships, by drawing them into direct participation in

---

* According to the *Directory,* the factories of European Russia in 1890 employed a total of 875,764 workers, of whom 210,207 (24%) were women, 17,793 (2%) boys, and 8,216 (1%) girls.

social production, large-scale machine industry stimulates their development and increases their independence, in other words, creates conditions of life that are incomparably superior to the patriarchal immobility of pre-capitalist relations.*

First written in 1896-99

First printed in book form
at the end of March 1899   *Collected Works*, Vol. 3

---

* "The poor woman-weaver follows her father and husband to the factory and works alongside of them and independently of them. She is as much a breadwinner as the man is." "In the factory ... the woman is quite an independent producer, apart from her husband." Literacy spreads among the women factory workers with remarkable rapidity. (*Industries of Vladimir Gubernia*, III, 113, 118, 112 and elsewhere.) Mr. Kharizomenov is perfectly right in drawing the following conclusion: industry has destroyed "the economic dependence of the woman on the family ... and on the husband.... At the factory, the woman is the equal of the man; this is the equality of the proletarian.... The capitalisation of industry is an important factor in the woman's struggle for her independence in the family." "Industry creates a new position for the woman in which she is completely independent of her family and husband." (*Yuridichesky Vestnik*, 1883, No. 12, pp. 582, 596.) In the *Statistical Returns for Moscow Gubernia* (Vol. VII, Pt. II, Moscow, 1882, pp. 152, 138-39), the investigators compare the position of women engaged in making stockings by hand and by machine. The daily earnings of hand workers is about 8 kopeks, and of machine workers, 14 to 30 kopeks. The working woman's conditions under machine production are described as follows: "...Before us is a free young woman, hampered by no obstacles, emancipated from the family and from all that constitutes the peasant woman's conditions of life, a young woman who at any moment may leave one place for another, one employer for another, and may at any moment find herself without a job ... without a crust of bread.... Under hand production, the knitter's earnings are very meagre, insufficient to cover the cost of her food, earnings only acceptable if she, as a member of an allotment-holding and farming family, enjoys in part the product of that land; under machine production the working woman, in addition to food and tea, gets earnings which enable ... her to live away from the family and to do without the family's income from the land.... Moreover, the woman worker's earnings in machine industry, under present conditions, are more secure."

FROM Draft Programme of the Russian Social-Democratic Labour Party[8]

[B]

XIII. The tsarist autocracy is the most outstanding of these remnants of the serf-owning system and the most formidable bulwark of all this barbarism. It is the bitterest and most dangerous enemy of the proletarian emancipation movement and the cultural development of the entire people.

[C]

For these reasons* the Russian Social-Democratic Labour Party advances as its immediate political task the overthrow of the tsarist autocracy and its replacement by a *republic* based on a democratic constitution that would ensure:

1) the people's sovereignty, i.e., concentration of supreme state power in the hands of a legislative assembly consisting of representatives of the people;

2) universal, equal, and direct suffrage, both in elections to the legislative assembly and in elections to all local organs of self-government, for every citizen who has reached the age of twenty-one; the secret ballot at all elections; the right of every voter to be elected to any of the representative assemblies; remuneration for representatives of the people;

3) inviolability of the person and domicile of citizens;

4) unrestricted freedom of conscience, speech, the press and of assembly, the right to strike and to organise unions;

---

* Here begins the text adopted by the committee as a whole.

5) freedom of movement and occupation;

6) abolition of social-estates; full equality for all citizens, irrespective of sex, religion or race;

7) recognition of the right to self-determination for all nations forming part of the state;

8) the right of every citizen to prosecute any official, without previously complaining to the latter's superiors;

9) general arming of the people instead of maintaining a standing army;

10) separation of the church from the state and of the school from the church;

11) universal, free, and compulsory education up to the age of sixteen; state provision of food, clothing, and school supplies to needy children.

[D]

To protect the working class and to raise its fighting capacity,* the Russian Social-Democratic Labour Party demands:

1) that the working day be limited to eight hours for all wage-workers;

2) that a weekly rest period of not less than thirty-six consecutive hours for wage-workers of both sexes employed in all branches of the national economy be established by law;

3) that all overtime be prohibited;

4) that night-work (from 9 p.m. to 5 a.m) in all branches of the national economy be prohibited, with the exception of those branches in which it is essential for technical reasons;

5) that employers be forbidden to employ children under the age of fifteen;

6) that female labour be forbidden in industries specifically injurious to the health of women;

7) that the law establish employers' civil liability for workers' complete or partial disability caused by accidents or by harmful working conditions; that the worker should not be required to prove his employer's responsibility for disability;

---

* Frey moved that the beginning of this paragraph be altered to read as follows: "To safeguard the working class from physical and moral degeneration, and also to raise its fighting capacity in the struggle for its emancipation...."

8) that payment of wages in kind be prohibited*;

9) that state pensions be paid to aged workers, who have become incapacitated;

10) that the number of factory inspectors be increased; that female inspectors be appointed in industries in which female labour predominates; that observance of the factory laws be supervised by representatives elected by the workers and paid by the state; piece rates and rejection of work done should also be supervised by elected representatives of the workers;

11) that local self-government bodies, in co-operation with elected representatives of the workers, supervise sanitary conditions in living quarters provided for workers by employers, and also see to the observance of rules operating in such living quarters and the terms on which they are leased, with the object of protecting the wage-workers from employers' interference in their lives and activities as private persons and citizens;

12) that a properly organised and comprehensive system of sanitary inspection be instituted to supervise working conditions at all enterprises employing wage-labour;

13) that the Factory Inspectorate's activities be extended to artisan, home, and handicraft industries, and to state-owned enterprises;

14) that any breach of the labour protection laws be punishable by law;

15) that employers be forbidden to make any deductions from wages, on any grounds or for any purpose whatsoever (fines, rejections, etc.);

16) that factory courts[9] be set up in all branches of the national economy, with equal representation of workers and employers.

Written in late January-
early February 1902

---

* Frey moved that the following be inserted here (in the same clause): "that the law should establish weekly payment for all workers employed on a contract basis."

FROM The International Socialist Congress in Stuttgart

The resolution on women's suffrage was also adopted unanimously. Only one Englishwoman from the semi-bourgeois Fabian Society[10] defended the admissibility of a struggle not for full women's suffrage but for one limited to those possessing property. The Congress rejected this unconditionally and declared in favour of women workers campaigning for the franchise, not in conjunction with the bourgeois supporters of women's rights, but in conjunction with the class parties of the proletariat. The Congress recognised that in the campaign for women's suffrage it was necessary to uphold fully the principles of socialism and equal rights for men and women without distorting those principles for the sake of expediency.

In this connection an interesting difference of opinion arose in the Commission. The Austrians (Viktor Adler, Adelheid Popp) justified their tactics in the struggle for universal manhood suffrage: for the sake of winning this suffrage, they thought it expedient in the campaign not to put the demand for women's suffrage, too, in the foreground. The German Social-Democrats, and especially Clara Zetkin, had protested against this when the Austrians were campaigning for universal suffrage. Zetkin declared in the press that they should not under any circumstances have neglected the demand for women's suffrage, that the Austrians had opportunistically sacrificed principle to expediency, and that they would not have narrowed the scope of their agitation, but would have widened it and increased the force of the popular movement had they fought for women's suffrage with the same energy. In the Commission Zetkin was supported whole-heartedly by another prominent German woman Social-Democrat, Zietz. Adler's amendment, which indirectly justified the Austrian tactics, was *rejected* by 12 votes to 9 (this amendment stated only that there should be no abatement of the struggle for a suffrage that would really extend to all citizens, instead of stating that the struggle for the suffrage should always include the demand for equal rights for men and women). The point of view of the Commission and of the Congress may be most accurately expressed in the following words of the above-mentioned Zietz in her speech at the International Socialist Women's Conference (this Conference took place in Stuttgart at the same time as the Congress):

"In principle we must demand all that we consider to be correct," said Zietz, "and only when our strength is inadequate for more, do we accept what we are able to get. That has always been the tactics of Social-Democracy. The more modest our demands the more modest will the government be in its concessions...." This controversy between the Austrian and German women Social-Democrats will enable the reader to see how severely the best Marxists treat the slightest deviation from the principles of consistent revolutionary tactics.

Written in September 1907

Published in September 1907   *Collected Works*, Vol. 13
in *Kalendar dlya vsekh, 1908*

Civilised Europeans
and Savage Asians

The well-known English Social-Democrat, Rothstein, relates in the German labour press an instructive and typical incident that occurred in British India. This incident reveals better than all arguments why the revolution is growing apace in that country with its more than 300 million inhabitants.

Arnold, a British journalist, who brings out a newspaper in Rangoon, a large town (with over 200,000 inhabitants) in one of the Indian provinces, published an article entitled: "A Mockery of British Justice." It exposed a local British judge named Andrew. For publishing this article Arnold was sentenced to twelve months' imprisonment, but he appealed and, having connections in London, was able to get the case before the highest court in Britain. The Government of India hastily "reduced" the sentence to four months and Arnold was released.

What was all the fuss about?

A British colonel named McCormick had a mistress whose servant was an eleven-year-old Indian girl, named Aina. This gallant representative of a civilised nation enticed Aina to his room, raped her and locked her up in his house.

It so happened that Aina's father was dying and he sent for his daughter. It was then that the village where he lived learned the whole story. The population seethed with indignation. The police were compelled to order McCormick's arrest.

But Judge Andrew released him on bail, and later acquitted him, following a disgraceful travesty of justice. The gallant colonel declared, as gentlemen of noble extraction usually do under such circumstances, that Aina was a prostitute, in proof of which he brought five witnesses. Eight witnesses, however, brought by Aina's mother were not even examined by Judge Andrew.

When the journalist Arnold was tried for libel, the President of the Court, Sir ("His Worship") Charles Fox, refused to allow him to call witnesses in his defence.

It must be clear to everyone that thousands and millions of such cases occur in India. Only absolutely exceptional circumstances enabled the "libeller" Arnold (the son of an influential London journalist) to get out of prison and secure publicity for the case.

Do not forget that the British Liberals put their "best" people at the head of the Indian administration. Not long ago the Viceroy of India, the chief of the McCormicks, Andrews and Foxes, was John Morley, the well-known radical author, a "luminary of European learning", a "most honourable man" in the eyes of all European and Russian liberals.

The "European" spirit has already awakened in Asia, the peoples of Asia have become democratic-minded.

Pravda No. 87, April 14, 1913   *Collected Works*, Vol. 19

A Great Technical Achievement

The world-famous British chemist, William Ramsay, has discovered a method of obtaining gas directly from a coal seam. Ramsay is already negotiating with a colliery owner on the practical application of this method.

A great modern technical problem is thus approaching solution. The revolution that will be effected by this solution will be a tremendous one.

At the present time, to utilise the energy contained in it, coal is transported all over the country and burned in numerous factories and homes.

Ramsay's discovery means a gigantic technical revolution in this, perhaps the most important, branch of production in capitalist countries.

Ramsay has discovered a method of transforming coal into gas right where the coal lies, without hauling it to the surface. A similar but much simpler method is sometimes used in the mining of salt: it is not brought to the surface directly, but is dissolved in water, the solution being pumped to the top.

Ramsay's method is to transform, as it were, the coal mines into enormous distilling apparatuses for the production of gas. Gas is used to drive gas engines which extract *twice as much* energy from coal as steam engines can. Gas engines, in their turn, transform the energy into electricity, which modern technology can already transmit over enormous distances.

Such a technical revolution would reduce the cost of electricity to *one-fifth* or even *one-tenth* of its present price. An enormous amount of human labour now spent in extracting and distributing coal would be saved. It would be possible to use even the poorest seams, now not being worked. The cost of lighting and heating houses would be greatly reduced.

This discovery will bring about an enormous revolution in industry.

But the consequences this revolution will have for social life as a whole under the present capitalist system will be quite different from those the discovery would yield under socialism.

Under capitalism the "release" of the labour of millions of miners engaged in extracting coal will inevitably cause mass unemployment, an enormous increase in poverty, and a worsening of the workers' conditions. And the profits of this great invention will be pocketed by the Morgans, Rockefellers, Ryabushinskys, Morozovs, and their suites of lawyers, directors, professors, and other flunkeys of capital.

Under socialism the application of Ramsay's method, which will "release" the labour of millions of miners, etc., will make it possible immediately to shorten the working day *for all* from 8 hours to, say, 7 hours and even less. The "electrification" of all factories and railways will make working conditions more hygienic, will free millions of workers from smoke, dust and dirt, and accelerate the transformation of dirty, repulsive workshops into clean, bright laboratories worthy of human beings. The electric lighting and heating of every home will relieve millions of "domestic slaves" of the need to spend three-fourths of their lives in smelly kitchens.

Capitalist technology is increasingly, day by day, *outgrowing* the social conditions which condemn the working people to wage-slavery.

Pravda No. 91, April 21, 1913   *Collected Works*, Vol. 19

Capitalism and Female Labour

Modern capitalist society is the hiding place of numerous cases of poverty and oppression that are not immediately visible. The scattered families of middle class people, artisans, factory workers, clerks and the lower civil servants, are indescribably poor and barely make ends meet in the *best* of times. Millions and millions of women in such families live (or rather drag out an existence) as household slaves, striving with a desperate daily effort to feed and clothe their families on a few coppers, economising in everything except their own labour.

It is from among these women that the capitalists are most eager to engage workers who work at home and who are prepared for a monstrously low wage to "earn" an extra crust of bread for themselves and their families. It is from among them that the capitalists of all countries (like the slave owners of antiquity and the feudal lords of the Middle Ages) choose any number of concubines at the most "favourable" price. No "moral indignation" (hypocritical in ninety-nine cases out of a hundred) about prostitution can do anything to prevent this commerce in women's bodies; as long as wage slavery exists, prostitution must inevitably continue. Throughout the history of society all the oppressed and exploited classes have always been compelled (their exploitation consists in this) to hand over to the oppressors, first, their unpaid labour and, secondly, their women to be the concubines of the "masters".

Slavery, feudalism and capitalism are alike in this respect. Only the *form* of the exploitation changes, the exploitation remains.

In Paris, the world capital, the centre of civilisation, an *exhibition* is now being held of the work of "exploited women workers employed in their homes".

Every exhibit bears a ticket showing how much the woman working at home *received* for making it and how much she could earn per day and per hour.

How does this work out? A woman working at home *cannot earn* more than one and a quarter francs, i.e., 50 kopeks, *on any article*. Most of the jobs pay wages that are immeasurably lower. Take lampshades, for instance— four kopeks a dozen. Or paper bags at 15 kopeks a thousand giving a wage of *six* kopeks an hour. And then there are little toys with ribbons, etc.—two and a half kopeks an hour; artificial flowers that bring in *two or three* kopeks an hour; and men's and women's underclothes—from *two* to six kopeks an hour. And so on ad infinitum.

Our workers' associations and trade unions should organise a similar "exhibition". It will not produce the tremendous profits obtained by bourgeois-organised exhibitions. An exhibition of proletarian women's poverty and want will bring benefits of another kind—it will help wage slaves, both men and women, to realise their condition, to take a look at their own "lives" and think about how to deliver themselves from this eternal oppression of poverty, want, prostitution and other humiliations suffered by the poor.

Written in April 27 (May 10), 1913

Published in *Pravda* No. 102, May 5, 1913

Collected Works, Vol. 23, 5th (Russian) edition

Published in English for the first time

The Working Class
and Neomalthusianism[11]

At the Pirogov Doctors' Congress[12] much interest was aroused and a long debate was held on the question of abortions. The report was made by Lichkus, who quoted figures on the exceedingly widespread practice of destroying the foetus in present-day so-called civilised states.

In New York, 80,000 abortions were performed in one year and in France there are as many as 36,000 every month. In St. Petersburg the percentage of abortions has more than doubled in five years.

The Pirogov Doctors' Congress adopted a resolution saying that there should never be any criminal prosecution of a mother for performing an artificial abortion and that doctors should only be prosecuted if the operation is performed for "purposes of gain".

In the discussion the majority agreed that abortions should not be punishable, and the question of the so-called neomalthusianism (the use of contraceptives) was naturally touched upon, as was also the social side of the matter. Mr. Vigdorchik, for instance, said, according to the report in *Russkoye Slovo*,[13] that "contraceptive measures should be welcomed" and Mr. Astrakhan exclaimed, amidst thunderous applause:

"We have to convince mothers to bear children so that they can be maimed in educational establishments, so that lots can be drawn for them, so that they can be driven to suicide!"

If the report is true that this exclamation of Mr. Astrakhan's was greeted with thunderous applause, it is a fact that does not surprise me. The audience was made up of bourgeois, middle and petty bourgeois, who have the psychology of the philistine. What can you expect from them but the most banal liberalism?

From the point of view of the working class, however, it would hardly be possible to find a more apposite expression of the completely reactionary nature and the ugliness of "social neomalthusianism" than Mr. Astrakhan's phrase cited above.

..."Bear children so that they can be maimed...." For that alone? Why not that they should *fight* better, more unitedly, consciously and resolutely than we are fighting against the present-day conditions of life that are maiming and ruining our generation?

This is the radical difference that distinguishes the psychology of the peasant, handicraftsman, intellectual, the petty bourgeois in general, from that of the proletarian. The petty bourgeois sees and feels that he is heading for ruin, that life is becoming more difficult, that the struggle for existence is ever more ruthless, and that his position and that of his family are becoming more and more hopeless. It is an indisputable fact, and the petty bourgeois protests against it.

But *how* does he protest?

He protests as the representative of a class that is hopelessly perishing, that despairs of its future, that is depressed and cowardly. There is nothing to be done ... if only there were fewer children to suffer our torments and hard toil, our poverty and our humiliation—such is the cry of the petty bourgeois.

The class-conscious worker is far from holding this point of view. He will not allow his consciousness to be dulled by such cries no matter how sincere and heartfelt they may be. Yes, we workers and the mass of small proprietors lead a life that is filled with unbearable oppression and suffering. Things are harder for our generation than they were for our fathers. But in one respect we are luckier than our fathers. *We have begun to learn and are rapidly learning to fight*—and to fight not as individuals, as the best of our fathers fought, not for the slogans of bourgeois speechifiers that are alien to us in spirit, but for our slogans, the slogans of our class. We are fighting better than our fathers did. Our children will fight better than we do, and *they will be victorious*.

The working class is not perishing, it is growing, becoming stronger, gaining courage, consolidating itself, educating itself and becoming steeled in battle. We are pessimists as far as serfdom, capitalism and petty production are concerned, but we are ardent optimists in what concerns the working-class movement and its aims. We are already laying the foundation of a new edifice and our children will complete its construction.

That is the reason—the only reason—why we are unconditionally the enemies of neomalthusianism, suited only to unfeeling and egotistic petty-bourgeois couples, who whisper in scared voices: "God grant we manage somehow by ourselves. So much the better if we have no children."

It goes without saying that this does not by any means prevent us from demanding the unconditional annulment of all laws against abortions or against the distribution of medical literature on contraceptive measures, etc. Such laws are nothing but the hypocrisy of the ruling classes. These laws do not heal the ulcers of capitalism, they merely turn them into malignant ulcers that are especially painful for the oppressed masses. Freedom for medical propaganda and the protection of the elementary democratic rights of citizens, men and women, are one thing. The social theory of neomalthusianism is quite another. Class-conscious workers will always conduct the most ruthless struggle against attempts to impose that reactionary and cowardly theory on the most progressive and strongest class in modern society, the class that is the best prepared for great changes.

Pravda No. 137, June 16, 1913   *Collected Works*, Vol. 19

Fifth International Congress
Against Prostitution

The *fifth* international congress for the suppression of the white slave traffic recently ended in London.

Duchesses, countesses, bishops, priests, rabbis, police officials and all sorts of bourgeois philanthropists were well to the fore! How many festive luncheons and magnificent official receptions were given! And how many solemn speeches on the harm and infamy of prostitution!

What means of struggle were proposed by the elegant bourgeois delegates to the congress? Mainly two methods—religion and police. They are, it appears, the most valid and reliable methods of combating prostitution. One English delegate boasted, according to the London correspondent of the *Leipziger Volkszeitung*,[14] that he had introduced a bill into parliament providing for *corporal punishment* for pimps. See the sort he is, this modern "civilised" hero of the struggle against prostitution!

One lady from Canada waxed enthusiastic over the police and the supervision of "fallen" women by policewomen, but as far as raising wages was concerned, she said that women workers did not deserve better pay.

One German pastor reviled present-day materialism, which, he said, is taking hold among the people and promoting the spread of free love.

When the Austrian delegate Gärtner tried to raise the question of the social causes of prostitution, of the need and poverty experienced by working-class families, of the exploitation of child labour, of unbearable housing conditions, etc., he was forced to silence by hostile shouts!

But the things that were said about highly-placed personages—among groups of delegates—were instructive and sublime. When, for example, the German Empress visits a maternity hospital in Berlin, *rings are placed on the fingers* of mothers of "illegitimate" children in order that this august individual may not be shocked by the sight of unmarried mothers!

We may judge from this of the disgusting bourgeois hypocrisy that reigns at these aristocratic-bourgeois congresses. Acrobats in the field of philanthropy and police defenders of this mockery of poverty and need gather "to struggle against prostitution", which is supported precisely by the aristocracy and the bourgeoisie. . . .

Rabochaya Pravda No. 1,
July 13, 1913

Collected Works, Vol. 19

Petty Production in Agriculture

The peasant question in modern capitalist states most
frequently gives rise to perplexity and vacillation among
Marxists and to most of the attacks on Marxism by bourgeois (professorial) political economy.

Petty production in agriculture is doomed to extinction
and to an incredibly abased and downtrodden position
under capitalism, say the Marxists. Petty production is
dependent on big capital, is backward in comparison with
large-scale production in agriculture, and can only keep
going by means of desperately reduced consumption and
laborious, arduous toil. The frittering away and waste of
human labour, the worst forms of dependence of the producer, exhaustion of the peasant's family, his cattle and his
land—this is what capitalism everywhere brings the peasant.

There is *no* salvation for the peasant except by joining in
the activities of the proletariat, primarily those of the wage-
workers.

Bourgeois political economy, and the Narodniks[15] and
opportunists who champion it (though they may not always
be conscious of the fact), on the contrary, try to prove that
petty production is viable and is more profitable than large-
scale production. The peasant, who has a firm and assured
position in capitalist society, must gravitate, not towards
the proletariat, but towards the bourgeoisie; he must not
gravitate towards the class struggle of the wage-workers
but must try to strengthen his position as a proprietor and
master—such, in substance, is the theory of the bourgeois
economists.

We will try to test the soundness of the proletarian and
bourgeois theories by means of precise data. Let us take

the data on *female* labour in agriculture in Austria and Germany. Full data for Russia are still lacking because the government is unwilling to take a scientifically based census of all agricultural enterprises.

In Austria, according to the census of 1902, out of 9,070,682 persons employed in agriculture 4,422,981, or 48.7 per cent, were women. In Germany, where capitalism is far more developed, women constitute the *majority* of those employed in agriculture—54.8 per cent. The more capitalism develops in agriculture the more it employs female labour, that is to say, *worsens* the living conditions of the working masses. Women employed in German industry make up 25 per cent of the total labour force, but in agriculture they constitute more than 50 per cent. This shows that industry is absorbing the *best* labour and leaving the weaker to agriculture.

In developed capitalist countries agriculture has already become mainly a women's occupation.

But if we examine statistics on farms of various sizes we shall see that it is in *petty* production that the exploitation of female labour assumes particularly large proportions. On the other hand, even in agriculture, large-scale capitalist production employs mainly male labour, although in this respect it has not caught up with industry.

The following are the comparative figures for Austria and Germany:

Type of farm	Group according to size of farm	Per cent of women employed	
		Austria	Germany
Proletarian	{ Up to half a hectare* { 1/2 to 2 hectares	52.0 50.9	74.1 65.7
Peasant	{ 2 to 5 " { 5 to 10 " { 10 to 20 "	49.6 48.5 48.6	54.4 50.2 48.4
Capitalist	{ 20 to 100 " { 100 hectares and over	46.6 27.4	44.8 41.0
For all farms		48.7	54.8

* One hectare=0.9 of a dessiatine, or 3.28 acres.—*Ed.*

34

In both countries we see the operation of the same law of capitalist agriculture. The smaller the scale of production the *poorer* is the composition of the labour force, and the greater the number of women among the total number of persons employed in agriculture.

The general situation under capitalism is the following. On proletarian farms, i.e., those whose "proprietors" live mainly by means of wage-labour (agricultural labourers, day-labourers, and wage-workers in general who possess a tiny plot of land), *female labour predominates over male labour,* sometimes to an enormous extent.

It must not be forgotten that the number of these proletarian or labourer farms is enormous: in Austria they amount to 1,300,000 out of a total of 2,800,000 farms, and in Germany there are even 3,400,000 out of a total of 5,700,000.

On peasant farms male and female labour is employed in nearly equal proportions.

Finally, on capitalist farms, male labour *predominates over female labour.*

What does this signify?

It signifies that the composition of the labour force in petty production is inferior to that in large-scale capitalist production.

It signifies that in agriculture the working woman—the proletarian woman and peasant woman—must exert herself ever so much more, must strain herself to the utmost, must toil at her work to the detriment of her health and the health of her children, in order to keep up as far as possible with the male worker in large-scale capitalist production.

It signifies that petty production keeps going under capitalism only by *squeezing out* of the worker a *larger* amount of work than is squeezed out of the worker in large-scale production.

The peasant is more tied up, more entangled in the complicated net of capitalist dependence than the wage-worker. He thinks he is independent, that he can "make good"; but as a matter of fact, in order to keep going, he must work (for capital) harder than the wage-worker.

The figures on *child* labour in agriculture prove this still more clearly.*

Rabochaya Pravda No. 5,   *Collected Works*, Vol. 19
July 18, 1913

* V. I. Lenin, *Collected Works*, Vol. 19, pp. 209-12.

To Inessa Armand ‹

Dear friend,
I advise you to write the plan of your pamphlet[16] in greater detail. Otherwise there is much that is unclear.

I feel bound to make one point right away. I suggest you delete altogether §3 dealing with "the demand (on the part of women) for free love".

This is, in fact, a bourgeois, not a proletarian, demand. What do you really mean by it? What *can* it be understood to mean?

1. Freedom *from* material (financial) considerations in love?

2. *From* material cares as well?

3. From religious prejudices?

4. From the ban imposed by one's father, etc.?

5. From the prejudices of "society"?

6. From the narrow surroundings of the (peasant or petty-bourgeois or intellectual-bourgeois) environment?

7. From the shackles of the law, the court and the police?

8. From earnestness in love?

9. From childbirth?

10. Freedom to commit adultery, etc.?

I have listed many (not all, of course) shades of meaning. You do not mean, of course, Nos. 8-10, but Nos. 1-7 or *something like* Nos. 1-7.

But for Nos. 1-7 another definition should be chosen, for free love does not express the idea exactly.

And the public at large, the readers will *inevitably* understand "free love" to mean in general something along the lines of Nos. 8-10, even *against your will*.

Precisely because in modern society the most talkative and noisy "top strata" mean by "free love" Nos. 8-10, this demand for free love is a bourgeois, not a proletarian demand.

Nos. 1 and 2 are most important to the proletariat, and then Nos. 1-7, but this, properly speaking, is not "free love".

What you *subjectively* "want to understand" by it does not matter. What matters is *the objective logic* of class relations in affairs of love.

Friendly shake hands!*

W. I.

Written January 17, 1915
in Berne

First published in 1939   *Collected Works*, Vol. 35
in the magazine *Bolshevik* No. 13

---

* The beginning and ending of the letter were written by Lenin in English.—*Tr.*

To Inessa Armand*

Dear friend,

Forgive me for replying so late. I intended to reply yesterday, but I was too busy and didn't have the time to write.

As for the plan of your pamphlet, I was of the opinion that "the demand for free love" was not clear and, whether you wished it or not (I emphasised this by saying: "it is a question of the objective class relations, not of your subjective wishes"), it would be a bourgeois and not a proletarian demand in the social setting of the time.

You disagree with this.

Well, let us consider the matter over again.

To make clear what is unclear, I listed about ten *possible* (and inevitable in the conditions of class strife) different interpretations and pointed out that interpretations 1-7, in my opinion, would be typical or characteristic for proletarian women, while interpretations 8-10 would be typical or characteristic for bourgeois women.

If you wished to refute this, you should have shown, first, that these interpretations are not correct (and then you should have advanced other interpretations or pointed out the wrong ones) or second, that they are incomplete (and then you should have added the missing ones) or, third, that the division into proletarian and bourgeois interpretations is different from mine.

You do none of these three things.

---

* Slightly abridged.—*Ed.*

You don't mention points 1-7 at all. So, you admit that they are correct (on the whole)? (What you write about prostitution among proletarian women and their dependence: "the impossibility of saying no" fully fits points 1-7. There is no cause for disagreement between us to be found here.)

Nor do you deny that it is a *proletarian* interpretation. Now there remain points 8-10.

You "don't quite understand" them and raise this "objection": "I don't see how one *could* (exactly what you wrote!) *identify* (!!??) free love with" point 10. . . .

And so, *I* "identify" the one with the other and you mean to shatter and destroy *me* for it.

Why? What for?

By free love *bourgeois women* mean points 8-10—such is my thesis.

Do you deny this thesis? Then say what *bourgeois* ladies mean by free love.

You keep silent about this. But do not literature and actual life *prove* that this is precisely what bourgeois women mean? They prove this to the hilt. And you tacitly admit it.

And if this is the case, it is a question of their class position, and it is hardly possible and rather naïve to "refute" *them*.

The proletarian point of view must be clearly *distinguished* from and *contrasted* with them. You should bear in mind the objective fact that otherwise *they* will tear the appropriate passages out of the context, interpret them in their own way and turn your pamphlet into grist for their mill; they will distort your ideas in the eyes of the workers and get them "muddled" (making them wonder if it is not *alien* ideas that *you* are advocating). And they have newspapers, etc., galore.

And you completely forget the objective and class point of view and "attack" *me,* accusing me of having "identified" "free love" with points 8-10. Strange, very strange indeed. . . .

"Even a short-lived passion and love affair" are "more poetic and more pure" than the "unloving kisses" of (vulgar and very vulgar) married people. This is what you write. And this is what you are going to write in your pamphlet. Fine.

Is this a logical antithesis? Unloving kisses between vulgar married people are *dirty*. I agree. They should be contrasted with ... with what?... The apparent reply is: with *loving* kisses. And you advance in contrast to them "short-lived" (why short-lived?) "passion" (why not love?)! It follows logically from this that unloving (short-lived) kisses are contrasted with unloving matrimonial kisses.... Strange. Would it not be better in a popular pamphlet to contrast the petty-bourgeois, intellectual or peasant (my point 6 or 5, I think) vulgar and dirty marriage without love to the proletarian civic marriage with love (and add, *if you must have it in*, that a short-lived passionate affair can be pure and can be dirty). In your pamphlet you have juxtaposition not of class *types*, but something in the nature of "an individual case", which is possible, of course. But is this a question of individual cases? The theme of a separate, individual case of dirty kisses in marriage and pure kisses in a short-lived love affair should be developed in a novel (for here the whole *point* would be in the *individual* setting, in analysing the *characters* and psychology of *given* types). But in a pamphlet?

You have quite well grasped my point about the quotation from Key being unsuitable, because you say it is "absurd" to play the role of "professors *ès* love". Exactly. And what about the role of professors *ès* short-lived, etc.?

Actually the last thing I want is polemics. I would gladly stop writing this letter and leave the matter for a talk with you. But I do want the pamphlet to be a good one, so that *nobody can* tear out phrases that are to your disadvantage (*one* phrase is enough sometimes to spoil everything...) and *mis*interpret you. I am sure that you wrote this, too "unwittingly", and I am sending this letter because correspondence, rather than talks, may make you go deeper into the plan of the pamphlet, which is a very important thing.

Haven't you got a French Socialist among your women acquaintances? Translate for her (as if from the English) my points 1-10 and your remarks about short-lived, etc., and look at her and listen to her carefully—conduct a small experiment to see what *outsiders* will say and to find out their impressions and also what they expect of the pamphlet.

> I shake your hand and wish you
> to have fewer headaches
> and a speedy recovery, *V. U.*

Written January 24, 1915 in Berne

First published in 1939   *Collected Works*, Vol. 35
in the magazine
Bolshevik No. 13

FROM A Caricature of Marxism
and Imperialist Economism

P. Kievsky does not understand the difference between "negative" slogans that stigmatise *political* evils and *economic* evils. The difference lies in the fact that certain economic evils are part of capitalism as such, whatever the political superstructure, and that it is *impossible* to eliminate them economically without eliminating capitalism itself. Not a single instance can be cited to disprove this. On the other hand, political evils represent a departure from democracy which, economically, is fully possible "on the basis of the existing system", i.e., capitalism, and by way of exception is being implemented under capitalism— certain aspects in one country, other aspects in another. Again, what the author fails to understand is precisely the fundamental conditions necessary for the implementation of democracy in general!

The same applies to the question of divorce. The reader will recall that it was first posed by Rosa Luxemburg in the discussion on the *national* question. She expressed the perfectly justified opinion that if we uphold autonomy within a state (for a definite region, area, etc.), we must, as centralist Social-Democrats, insist that all major national issues—and *divorce* legislation is one of them—should come within the jurisdiction of the central government and central parliament. This example clearly demonstrates that one cannot be a democrat and socialist without demanding full freedom of divorce now, because the lack of such freedom is additional oppression of the oppressed sex—though it should not be difficult to realise that recognition of the *freedom* to leave one's husband is not an *invitation* to all wives to do so!

P. Kievsky "objects":

"What would this right [of divorce] be like if in *such* cases [when the wife *wants* to leave the husband] she could *not* exercise her right? Or if its exercise depended on the will of *third* parties, or, worse still, on the will of claimants to her affections? Would we advocate the proclamation of *such* a right? Of course not!"

That objection reveals complete failure to understand the relation between democracy *in general* and capitalism. The conditions that make it impossible for the oppressed classes to "exercise" their democratic rights are not the exception under capitalism; they are typical of the system. In most cases the right of divorce will remain unrealisable under capitalism, for the oppressed sex is subjugated economically. No matter how much democracy there is under capitalism, the woman remains a "domestic slave", a slave locked up in the bedroom, nursery, kitchen. The right to elect their "own" people's judges, officials, school-teachers, jurymen, etc., is likewise in most cases unrealisable under capitalism precisely because of the economic subjection of the workers and peasants. The same applies to the democratic republic: our programme defines it as "government by the people", though all Social-Democrats know perfectly well that under capitalism, even in the most democratic republic there is bound to be bribery of officials by the bourgeoisie and an alliance of stock exchange and the government.

Only those who cannot think straight or have no knowledge of Marxism will conclude: so there is no point in having a republic, no point in freedom of divorce, no point in democracy, no point in self-determination of nations! But Marxists know that democracy does *not* abolish class oppression. It only makes the class struggle more direct, wider, more open and pronounced, and that is what we need. The fuller the freedom of divorce, the clearer will women see that the source of their "domestic slavery" is capitalism, not lack of rights. The more democratic the system of government, the clearer will the workers see that the root evil is capitalism, not lack of rights. The fuller national equality (and it is *not* complete without freedom of secession), the clearer will the workers of the oppressed nations see that the cause of their oppression is capitalism, not lack of rights, etc.

It must be said again and again: It is embarrassing to have to drive home the ABC of Marxism, but what is one to do if Kievsky does not know it?

He discusses divorce in much the same way as one of the secretaries of the Organising Committee[17] abroad, Semkovsky, discussed it, if I remember rightly, in the Paris *Golos*.[18] His line of reasoning was that freedom of divorce is not, it is true, an invitation to all wives to leave their husbands, but if it is proved that all other husbands are better than yours, madame, then it amounts to one and the same thing!!

In taking that line of argument Semkovsky forgot that crank thinking is not a violation of socialist or democratic principles. If Semkovsky were to tell a woman that all other husbands are better than hers, no one would regard this as violation of democratic principles. At most people would say: There are bound to be big cranks in a big party! But if Semkovsky were to take it into his head to defend as a democrat a person who opposed freedom of divorce and appealed, for instance, to the courts, the police or the church to prevent his wife leaving him, we feel sure that *even* most of Semkovsky's colleagues on the Secretariat Abroad, though they are sorry socialists, would refuse to support him!

Both Semkovsky and Kievsky, in their "discussion" of divorce, fail to understand the issue and avoid its substance, namely, that under capitalism the right of divorce, as *all* other democratic rights without exception, is conditional, restricted, formal, narrow and extremely difficult of realisation. Yet no self-respecting Social-Democrat will consider anyone opposing the right of divorce a democrat, let alone a socialist. That is the crux of the matter. *All* "democracy" consists in the proclamation and realisation of "rights" which under capitalism are realisable only to a very small degree and only relatively. But without the proclamation of these rights, without a struggle to introduce them now, immediately, without training the masses in the spirit of this struggle, socialism is *impossible*.

Written August-October 1916

First published in *Zvezda*
Nos. 1 and 2, 1924

Collected Works, Vol. 23

**FROM Tasks of the Left Zimmerwaldists
in the Swiss Social-Democratic Party**[19]

**III. Pressing Democratic Reforms
and Utilisation
of the Political Struggle
and Parliamentarism**

17. Abolition of *all* restrictions without exception on the political rights of women compared with those of men. It must be explained to the masses why this reform is particularly urgent at the present time, when the war and the high cost of living are agitating the minds of the broad masses and, in particular, are rousing the interest and the attention of women towards politics.

Written in late October
and early November 1916

First published in French   *Collected Works*, Vol. 23
as a pamphlet in 1918

FROM The Tasks of the Proletariat in Our Revolution

12. The substitution of a people's militia for the police is a reform that follows from the entire course of the revolution and that is now being introduced in most parts of Russia. We must explain to the people that in most of the bourgeois revolutions of the usual type, this reform was always extremely short-lived, and that the bourgeoisie—even the most democratic and republican—restored the police of the old, tsarist type, a police divorced from the people, commanded by the bourgeoisie and capable of oppressing the people in every way.

There is only one way to *prevent* the restoration of the police, and that is to create a people's militia and to fuse it with the army (the standing army to be replaced by the arming of the entire people). Service in this militia should extend to all citizens of both sexes between the ages of fifteen and sixty-five without exception, if these tentatively suggested age limits may be taken as indicating the participation of adolescents and old people. Capitalists must pay their workers, servants, etc., for days devoted to public service in the militia. Unless women are brought to take an independent part not only in political life generally, but also in daily and universal public service, it is no use talking about full and stable democracy, let alone socialism. And such "police" functions as care of the sick and of homeless children, food inspection, etc., will never be satisfactorily discharged until women are on an equal footing with men, not merely nominally but in reality.

The tasks which the proletariat must put before the people in order to safeguard, consolidate and develop the revolution are to prevent the restoration of the police and to enlist the organisational forces of the entire people in forming a people's militia.

First published September 1917   *Collected Works*, Vol. 24
as a pamphlet by *Priboi* Publishers

FROM Materials
Relating to the Revision
of the Party Programme[20]

The constitution of the Russian democratic republic must ensure:

1) The sovereignty of the people; supreme power in the state must be vested entirely in the people's representatives, who shall be elected by the people and be subject to recall at any time, and who shall constitute a single popular assembly, a single chamber.

1) The sovereignty of the people, i.e., the concentration of supreme state power in the hands of a legislative assembly, consisting of the representatives of the people and constituting a single chamber.

2) Universal, equal, and direct suffrage for all citizens, men and women, who have reached the age of twenty, in the elections to the legislative assembly and to the various bodies of local self-government; secret ballot; the right of every voter to be elected to any representative institution; biennial parliaments; salaries to be paid to the people's representatives; **proportional representation at all elections; all delegates and elected officials, without exception, to be subject to recall at any time upon the decision of a majority of their electors.**

3) Local self-government on a broad scale; regional self-government in localities where the composition of the population and living and social conditions are of a specific nature; **the abolition of all state-appointed local and regional authorities.**

4) Inviolability of person and domicile.

5) Unrestricted freedom of conscience, speech, the press, assembly, strikes, and association.

6) Freedom of movement and occupation.

7) Abolition of the social-estates; equal rights for all citizens irrespective of sex, creed, race, or nationality.

8) The right of the population to receive instruction in their native tongue in schools to be established for the purpose at the expense of the state and local organs of self-government; the right of every citizen to use his native language at meetings; the native language to be used *on a level with the official language* in all local public and state institutions; **obligatory official language to be abolished.**

9) The right of self-determination for all member nations of the state.

9) The right of all member nations of the state to freely secede and form independent states. The republic of the Russian nation must attract other nations or nationalities not by force, but exclusively by voluntary agreement to form a common state. The unity and fraternal alliance of the workers of all countries is incompatible with the use of force, direct or indirect, against other nationalities.

10) The right of all persons to sue any official in the regular way before a jury.

11) Election of judges by the people.

11) Judges and other officials, both civil and military, to be elected by the people with the right to recall any of them at any time by decision of a majority of their electors.

12) Replacement of the standing army by the universally armed people.

12) The police and standing army to be replaced by the universally armed people; workers and other employees to receive regular wages from the capitalists for the time devoted to public service in the people's militia.

13) Separation of the church from the state, and schools from the church; schools to be absolutely secular.

14) Free and compulsory general and vocational education for all children of both sexes up to the age of sixteen; poor children to be provided with food, clothing, and school supplies at the expense of the state.

14) Free and compulsory general and polytechnical

education (familiarising the student with the theoretical and practical aspects of the most important fields of production) for all children of both sexes up to the age of sixteen; training of children to be closely integrated with socially productive work.

15) All students to be provided with food, clothing, and school supplies at the cost of the state.

16) Public education to be administered by democratically elected organs of local self-government; the central government not to be allowed to interfere with the arrangement of the school curriculum, or with the selection of the teaching staffs; teachers to be elected directly by the population with the right of the latter to remove undesirable teachers.

As a basic condition for the democratisation of our country's national economy, the Russian Social-Democratic Labour Party demands the abolition of all indirect taxes and the establishment of a progressive tax on incomes and inheritances.

The high level of development of capitalism already achieved in banking and in the trustified branches of industry, on the one hand, and the economic disruption caused by the imperialist war, everywhere evoking a demand for state and public control of the production and distribution of all staple products, on the other, induce the Party to demand the nationalisation of the banks, syndicates (trusts), etc.

To safeguard the working class from physical and moral deterioration, and develop its ability to carry on the struggle for emancipation, the Party demands:

1) An eight-hour working day for all wage-workers.

1) An eight-hour working day for all wage-workers, including a break of not less than one hour for meals where work is continuous. In dangerous and unhealthy industries the working day to be reduced to from four to six hours.

2) A statutory weekly uninterrupted rest period of not less than forty-two hours for all wage-workers of both sexes in all branches of the national economy.

3) Complete prohibition of overtime work.

4) Prohibition of night-work (from 9 p.m. to 6 a.m.) in all branches of the national economy except in cases where it is absolutely necessary for technical reasons endorsed by the labour organisations.

4) Prohibition of night-work (from 8 p.m. to 6 a.m.) in all branches of the national economy except in cases where it is absolutely necessary for technical reasons endorsed by the labour organisations—provided, however, that night-work does not exceed four hours.

5) Prohibition of the employment of children of school-age (under sixteen) and restriction of the working day of adolescents (from sixteen to eighteen) to six hours.

5) Prohibition of the employment of children of school-age (under sixteen), restriction of the working day of adolescents (from sixteen to twenty) to four hours, and prohibition of the employment of adolescents on night-work in unhealthy industries and mines.

6) Prohibition of female labour in all branches of industry injurious to women's health; women to be released from work for four weeks before and six weeks after child-birth, without loss of pay.

6) Prohibition of female labour in all branches of industry injurious to women's health; prohibition of night work for women; women to be released from work eight weeks before and eight weeks after child-birth, without loss of pay and with free medical and medicinal aid.

7) Establishment of nurseries for infants and young children at all factories and other enterprises where women are employed; nursing mothers to be allowed recesses of at least half-hour duration at intervals of not more than three hours.

7) Establishment of nurseries for infants and young children and rooms for nursing mothers at all factories and other enterprises where women are employed; nursing mothers to be allowed recesses of at least half-hour duration at intervals of not more than three hours; such mothers to receive nursing benefit and their working day to be reduced to six hours.

8) State insurance for workers covering old age and total or partial disablement out of a special fund formed by a special tax on the capitalists.

8) Full social insurance of workers:
a) for all forms of wage-labour;
b) for all forms of disablement, namely, sickness, injury, infirmity, old age, occupational disease, child-birth, widowhood, orphanhood, and also unemployment, etc.;

c) all insurance institutions to be administered entirely by the insured themselves;

d) the cost of insurance to be borne by the capitalists;

e) free medical and medicinal aid under the control of self-governing sick benefit societies, the management bodies of which are to be elected by the workers.

9) Payment of wages in kind to be prohibited; regular weekly pay-days to be fixed in all labour contracts without exception and wages to be paid in cash and during working hours.

10) Prohibition of deductions by employers from wages on any pretext or for any purpose whatsoever (fines, spoilage, etc.).

11) Appointment of an adequate number of factory inspectors in all branches of the national economy; factory inspection to be extended to all enterprises employing hired labour, including government enterprises (domestic service also to be liable to inspection); women inspectors to be appointed in industries where female labour is employed; representatives elected by the workers and paid by the state to supervise the enforcement of the factory laws, the fixing of rates and the passing or rejection of raw materials and finished products.

9) The establishment of a labour inspectorate elected by the workers' organisations and covering all enterprises employing hired labour, as well as domestic servants; women inspectors to be appointed in enterprises where female labour is employed.

Written in April-May 1917

Published in June 1917
in the pamphlet *Materials
Relating to the Revision
of the Party Programme*,
Priboi Publishers, Petrograd

Collected Works, Vol. 24

FROM Can the Bolsheviks Retain State Power?

The proletariat, we are told, will not be able to set the state apparatus in motion.

Since the 1905 Revolution, Russia has been governed by 130,000 landowners, who have perpetrated endless violence against 150,000,000 people, heaped unconstrained abuse upon them, and condemned the vast majority to inhuman toil and semi-starvation.

Yet we are told that the 240,000 members of the Bolshevik Party will not be able to govern Russia, govern her in the interests of the poor and against the rich. These 240,000 are already backed by no less than a million votes of the adult population, for this is precisely the proportion between the number of Party members and the number of votes cast for the Party that has been established by the experience of Europe and the experience of Russia as shown, for example, by the elections to the Petrograd City Council last August. We therefore already have a "state apparatus" of *one million* people devoted to the socialist state for the sake of high ideals and not for the sake of a fat sum received on the 20th of every month.

In addition to that we have a "magic way" to enlarge our state apparatus *tenfold* at once, at one stroke, a way which no capitalist state ever possessed or could possess. This magic way is to draw the working people, to draw the poor, into the daily work of state administration.

To explain how easy it will be to employ this magic way and how faultlessly it will operate, let us take the simplest and most striking example possible.

The state is to forcibly evict a certain family from a flat and move another in. This often happens in the capitalist state, and it will also happen in our proletarian or socialist state.

The capitalist state evicts a working-class family which has lost its breadwinner and cannot pay the rent. The bailiff appears with police, or militia, a whole squad of them. To effect an eviction in a working-class district a whole detachment of Cossacks is required. Why? Because the bailiff and the militiaman refuse to go without a very strong military guard. They know that the scene of an eviction arouses such fury among the neighbours, among thousands and thousands of people who have been driven to the verge of desperation, arouses such hatred towards the capitalists and the capitalist state, that the bailiff and the squad of militiamen run the risk of being torn to pieces at any minute. Large military forces are required, several regiments must be brought into a big city, and the troops must come from some distant, outlying region so that the soldiers will not be familiar with the life of the urban poor, so that the soldiers will not be "infected" with socialism.

The proletarian state has to forcibly move a very poor family into a rich man's flat. Let us suppose that our squad of workers' militia is fifteen strong: two sailors, two soldiers, two class-conscious workers (of whom, let us suppose, only one is a member of our Party, or a sympathiser), one intellectual, and eight from the poor working people, of whom at least five must be women, domestic servants, unskilled labourers, and so forth. The squad arrives at the rich man's flat, inspects it and finds that it consists of five rooms occupied by two men and two women—"You must squeeze up a bit into two rooms this winter, citizens, and prepare two rooms for two families now living in cellars. Until the time when, with the aid of engineers (you are an engineer, aren't you?), we have built good dwellings for everybody, you will have to squeeze up a little. Your telephone will serve ten families. This will save a hundred hours of work wasted on shopping, and so forth. Now in your family there are two unemployed persons who can perform light work: a citizeness fifty-five years of age and a citizen fourteen years of age. They will be on duty for three hours a day supervising the proper distribution of provisions for ten families and keeping the necessary account of this. The student citizen in our squad will now write out this state order in two copies and you will be kind enough to give us a signed declaration that you will faithfully carry it out."

This, in my opinion, shows, by means of striking examples, how the distinction between the old bourgeois and the new socialist state apparatus and state administration could be illustrated.

We are not utopians. We know that an unskilled labourer or a cook cannot immediately get on with the job of state administration. In this we agree with the Cadets, with Breshkovskaya, and with Tsereteli. We differ, however, from these citizens in that we demand an immediate break with the prejudiced view that only the rich, or officials chosen from rich families, are capable of *administering* the state, of performing the ordinary, everyday work of administration. We demand that *training* in the work of state administration be conducted by class-conscious workers and soldiers and that this training be begun at once, i.e., that a *beginning* be made at once in training all the working people, all the poor, for this work.

We know that the Cadets are also willing to teach the people democracy. Cadet ladies are willing to deliver lectures to domestic servants on equal rights for women in accordance with the best English and French sources. And also, at the very next concert-meeting, before an audience of thousands, an exchange of kisses will be arranged on the platform: the Cadet lady lecturer will kiss Breshkovskaya, Breshkovskaya will kiss ex-Minister Tsereteli, and the grateful people will therefore receive an object-lesson in republican equality, liberty and fraternity. . . .

Yes, we agree that the Cadets, Breshkovskaya and Tsereteli are in their own way devoted to democracy and are propagating it among the people. But what is to be done if our conception of democracy is somewhat different from theirs?

In our opinion, to ease the incredible burdens and miseries of the war and also to heal the terrible wounds the war has inflicted on the people, *revolutionary* democracy is needed, *revolutionary* measures of the kind described in the example of the distribution of housing accommodation in the interests of the poor. Exactly the same procedure must be adopted in both town and country for the distribution of provisions, clothing, footwear, etc., in respect of the land in the rural districts, and so forth. For the administration of the state in *this* spirit we can *at once set in motion a state* apparatus consisting of ten if not twenty million people, an apparatus such as no capitalist state has ever known. We alone can create such an apparatus, for we are sure of the fullest and devoted sympathy of the vast majority of the population. We alone can create such an apparatus, because we have class-conscious workers disciplined by long capitalist "schooling" (it was not for nothing that we went to learn in the school of capitalism), workers who are *capable* of forming a workers' militia and of *gradually* expanding it (beginning to expand it at once) into a militia *embracing the whole people*. The class-conscious workers must lead, but for the work of administration they can enlist the vast mass of the working and oppressed people.

It goes without saying that this new apparatus is bound to make mistakes in taking its first steps. But did not the peasants make mistakes when they emerged from serfdom and began to manage their own affairs? Is there any way other than practice by which the people can learn to govern themselves and to avoid mistakes? Is there any way other than by proceeding immediately to genuine self-government by the people? The chief thing now is to abandon the prejudiced bourgeois-intellectualist view that only special officials, who by their very social position are entirely dependent upon capital, can administer the state. The chief thing is to put an end to the state of affairs in which bourgeois officials and "socialist" ministers are trying to govern in the old way but are incapable of doing so and, after seven months, are faced with a peasant revolt in a peasant country! The chief thing is to imbue the oppressed and working people with confidence in their own strength, to prove to them in practice that they can and must themselves undertake the *proper*, most strictly regulated and organised distribution of bread, all kinds of food, milk, clothing, housing, etc., *in the interests of the poor*. Unless this is done, Russia *cannot* be saved from collapse and ruin. The conscientious, bold, universal move to hand over administrative work to proletarians and semi-proletarians, will rouse such unprecedented revolutionary enthusiasm among the people, will so multiply the people's forces in combating distress, that much that seemed impossible to our narrow, old, bureaucratic forces will become possible for the millions, who will *begin to work for themselves* and not for the capitalists, the gentry, the bureaucrats, and not out of fear of punishment.

* * *

To fear the resistance of the capitalists and yet to call oneself a revolutionary, to wish to be regarded as a socialist—isn't that disgraceful? How low must international socialism, corrupted by opportunism, have fallen ideologically if such voices *could* be raised!

We have already seen the strength of the capitalists' resistance; the entire people have seen it, for the capitalists are more class-conscious than the other classes and at once realised the significance of the Soviets, at once exerted *all their efforts* to the utmost, resorted to everything, went to all lengths, resorted to the most incredible lies and slander, to military plots in order to *frustrate the Soviets*, to reduce them to nought, to prostitute them (with the aid of the Mensheviks and Socialist-Revolutionaries[21]), to transform them into talking-shops, to wear down the peasants and workers by months and months of empty talk and playing at revolution.

We have not yet seen, however, the strength of resistance of the proletarians and poor peasants, for this strength will become fully apparent only when power is in the hands of the proletariat, when tens of millions of people who have been crushed by want and capitalist slavery see from experience and *feel* that state power has passed into the hands of the oppressed classes, that the state is helping the poor to fight the landowners and capitalists, is *breaking* their resistance. *Only* then shall we see what untapped forces of resistance to the capitalists are latent among the people; only then will what Engels called "latent socialism" manifest itself. Only then, for every *ten thousand* overt and concealed enemies of working-class rule, manifesting themselves actively or by passive resistance, there will arise *a million* new fighters who have been politically dormant, suffering in the torments of poverty and despair, having ceased to believe that they are human, that they have the right to live, that they too can be served by the entire might of the modern centralised state, that *their* contingents of the proletarian militia can, with the fullest confidence, also be called upon to take a direct, immediate, daily part in state administration.

The capitalists and landowners, with the benevolent assistance of Plekhanov, Breshkovskaya, Tsereteli, Chernov and Co., have done *everything* in their power to *defile* the democratic republic, to defile it by servility to wealth to such a degree that the people are being overcome by apathy, indifference; *it is all the same to them*, because the hungry man cannot see the difference between the republic and the monarchy; the freezing, barefooted, worn-out soldier sacrificing his life for alien interests is not able to love the republic.

But when every labourer, every unemployed worker, every cook, every ruined peasant sees, not from the newspapers, but with his own eyes, that the proletarian state is not cringing to wealth but is helping the poor, that this state does not hesitate to adopt revolutionary measures, that it confiscates surplus stocks of provisions from the parasites and distributes them to the hungry, that it forcibly installs the homeless in the houses of the rich, that it compels the rich to pay for milk but does not give them a drop until the children of *all* poor families are sufficiently supplied, that the land is being transferred to the working people and the factories and banks are being placed under the control of the workers and that immediate and severe punishment is meted out to the millionaires who conceal their wealth—when the poor see and feel this, no capitalist or kulak forces, no forces of world finance capital which manipulates thousands of millions, will vanquish the people's revolution; on the contrary, *the socialist revolution* will triumph all over the world for it is maturing in all countries.

Our revolution will be invincible if it is not afraid of itself, if it transfers all power to the proletariat, for behind us stand the immeasurably larger, more developed, more organised world forces of the proletariat which are temporarily held down by the war but not destroyed; on the contrary, the war has multiplied them.

Written at the end of
September-October 1 (14), 1917
Published in the magazine
Prosveshcheniye
No. 1-2, October 1917

Collected Works, Vol. 26

Speech
at the First All-Russia Congress
of Working Women
November 19, 1918[22]

Comrades, in a certain sense this congress of the women's section of the workers' army has a special significance, because one of the hardest things in every country has been to stir the women into action. There can be no socialist revolution unless very many working women take a big part in it.

No wonder women are called domestic slaves: such is the status of women in all civilised countries, even the most advanced. Women do not enjoy full equality in any capitalist state, not even in the freest of republics.

One of the first tasks of the Soviet Republic is to abolish all restrictions on women's rights. The Soviet government has completely abolished divorce proceedings, that source of bourgeois degradation, repression and humiliation.

It will soon be a year now since complete freedom of divorce was legislated. We have passed a decree annulling all distinction between legitimate and illegitimate children and removing several political restrictions. Nowhere else in the world have equality and freedom for working women been so fully established.

We know that it is the working-class woman who has to bear the full brunt of antiquated codes.

For the first time in history, our law has removed everything that denied women rights. But the important thing is not the law. In the cities and industrial areas this law on complete freedom of marriage is doing all right, but in the countryside it all too frequently remains a dead letter. There the religious marriage still predominates. This is due to the influence of the priests, an evil that is harder to combat than the old legislation.

We must be extremely careful in fighting religious prejudices; some people cause a lot of harm in this struggle by offending religious feelings. We must use propaganda and education. By lending too sharp an edge to the struggle we may only arouse popular resentment; such methods of struggle tend to perpetuate the division of the people along religious lines, whereas our strength lies in unity. The deepest source of religious prejudice is poverty and ignorance; and that is the evil we have to combat.

The status of women up to now has been compared to that of a slave; women have been tied to the home, and only socialism can save them from this. They will only be completely emancipated when we can get rid of the small peasant farms to proceed to co-operative farming and use collective methods to work the land. That is a difficult task. But now that Poor Peasant Committees[23] are being formed, the time has come when the socialist revolution is being consolidated.

The poorest part of the rural population is only now beginning to organise, but socialism is acquiring a firm foundation in these organisations of poor peasants.

Before, often the town became revolutionary and then the countryside.

But the present revolution relies on the countryside, and therein lie its significance and strength. The experience of all liberation movements has shown that the success of a revolution depends on how much the women take part in it. The Soviet government is doing everything in its power to enable women to carry on independent proletarian socialist work.

The Soviet government is in a difficult situation because the imperialists of all countries hate Soviet Russia and are preparing to go to war with her for kindling the fire of revolution in a number of countries and for taking determined steps towards socialism.

Now that they are out to destroy revolutionary Russia, the ground is beginning to burn under their own feet. You know how the revolutionary movement is spreading in

Germany. In Denmark the workers are fighting their government. In Holland and Switzerland the revolutionary movement is getting stronger. The revolutionary movement in these small countries has no importance in itself, but it is particularly significant because there was no war in these countries and they had the most "constitutional" democratic system. If countries like these are stirring into action, it makes us sure the revolutionary movement is taking a hold all over the world.

No other republic has so far been able to emancipate woman. The Soviet government is helping her. Our cause is invincible because the invincible working class is rising in all countries. This movement signifies the spread of the invincible socialist revolution. (*Prolonged applause. All sing the "Internationale".*)

Newspaper report, published
November 20, 1918
in *Izvestia* No. 253

Collected Works, Vol. 28

FROM Draft Programme of the R.C.P.(B.)[24]

First Paragraph of Section of Programme on the Courts

As it advances to communism through the dictatorship of the proletariat, the Communist Party, rejecting democratic slogans, completely abolishes also such organs of bourgeois rule as the old courts and replaces them by class courts of workers and peasants. After taking all power into its hands, the proletariat puts forward, instead of the old vague formula, "Election of judges by the people", the class slogan, "Election of judges from the working people by none but the working people", and carries it into practice throughout the judicial system. With regard to the election of judges from workers and peasants only who do not employ wage labour for profit, the Communist Party makes no distinction on account of sex but allows men and women completely equal rights both in electing judges and in exercising judicial functions. Having repealed the laws of the overthrown governments, the Party calls on the judges elected by Soviet electors to enforce the will of the proletariat and apply its decrees or, in the absence of relevant decrees, or if they are inadequate, to take guidance from their socialist sense of justice, ignoring the laws of the overthrown governments.

First published in 1930

Collected Works, Vol. 29

FROM A Great Beginning

Heroism of the Workers in the Rear
"Communist Subbotniks"[25]

We must all admit that vestiges of the bourgeois-intel-lectual phrasemongering approach to questions of the revo-lution are in evidence at every step, everywhere, even in our own ranks. Our press, for example, does little to fight these rotten survivals of the rotten bourgeois-democratic past; it does little to foster the simple, modest, ordinary but virile shoots of genuine communism.

Take the position of women. In this field, not a single democratic party in the world, not even in the most advanced bourgeois republic, has done in decades so much as a hundredth part of what we did in our very first year in power. We actually razed to the ground the infamous laws placing women in a position of inequality, restricting divorce and surrounding it with disgusting formalities, denying recognition to children born out of wedlock, enforcing a search for their fathers, etc., laws numerous survivals of which, to the shame of the bourgeoisie and of capitalism, are to be found in all civilised countries. We have a thousand times the right to be proud of what we have done in this field. But the more *thoroughly* we clear the ground of the lumber of the old, bourgeois laws and institutions, the more we realise that we have only cleared the ground to build on, but are not yet building.

Notwithstanding all the laws emancipating woman, she continues to be a *domestic slave*, because *petty housework* crushes, strangles, stultifies and degrades her, chains her to the kitchen and the nursery, and she wastes her labour on barbarously unproductive, petty, nerve-racking, stultifying and crushing drudgery. The real *emancipation of women*, real communism, will begin only where and when an all-out struggle begins (led by the proletariat wielding the state power) against this petty housekeeping, or rather when its *wholesale transformation* into a large-scale socialist economy begins.

Do we in practice pay sufficient attention to this question, which in theory every Communist considers indisputable? Of course not. Do we take proper care of the *shoots* of communism which already exist in this sphere? Again the answer is *no*. Public catering establishments, nurseries, kindergartens—here we have examples of these shoots, here we have the simple, everyday means, involving nothing pompous, grandiloquent or ceremonial, which can *really emancipate women*, really lessen and abolish their inequality with men as regards their role in social production and public life. These means are not new, they (like all the material prerequisites for socialism) were created by large-scale capitalism. But under capitalism they remained, first, a rarity, and secondly—which is particularly important—either *profit-making* enterprises, with all the worst features of speculation, profiteering, cheating and fraud, or "acrobatics of bourgeois charity", which the best workers rightly hated and despised.

There is no doubt that the number of these institutions in our country has increased enormously and that they are *beginning* to change in character. There is no doubt that we have far more *organising talent* among the women workers and peasant women than we are aware of, that we have far more people than we know of who can organise practical work, with the co-operation of large numbers of workers and of still larger numbers of consumers, without the abundance of talk, fuss, squabbling and chatter about plans, systems, etc., with which our big-headed "intellectuals" or half-baked "Communists" are "affected". But we *do not nurse* these shoots of the new as we should.

Look at the bourgeoisie. How very well they know how to advertise what *they* need! See how millions of copies of *their* newspapers extol what the capitalists regard as "model" enterprises, and how "model" bourgeois institutions are made an object of national pride! Our press does not take the trouble, or hardly ever, to describe the best catering establishments or nurseries, in order, by daily insistence, to get some of them turned into models of their kind. It does not give them enough publicity, does not describe in detail the saving in human labour, the conveniences for the consumer, the economy of products, the emancipation of women from domestic slavery, the improvement in sanitary conditions, that is achieved with *exemplary communist work*, that can be achieved and can be extended to the whole of society, to all working people.

Exemplary production, exemplary communist subbotniks, exemplary care and conscientiousness in procuring and distributing every pood of grain, exemplary catering establishments, exemplary cleanliness in such-and-such a workers' house, in such-and-such a block, should all receive ten times more attention and care from our press, as well as from *every* workers' and peasants' organisation, than they receive now. All these are shoots of communism, and it is our common and primary duty to nurse them. Difficult as our food and production situation is, in the eighteen months of Bolshevik rule there has been undoubted progress *all along the line*: grain procurements have increased from 30 million poods (from August 1, 1917, to August 1, 1918) to 100 million poods[26] (from August 1, 1918, to May 1, 1919); vegetable gardening has expanded, the margin of unsown land has diminished, railway transport has begun to improve despite the enormous fuel difficulties, and so on. Against this general background and with the support of the proletarian state power, the shoots of communism will not wither; they will grow and blossom into complete communism.

Published as a pamphlet
in July 1919, Moscow

The Tasks
of the Working Women's Movement
in the Soviet Republic

**Speech Delivered at the Fourth Moscow City Conference
of Non-Party Working Women
September 23, 1919**

Comrades, it gives me pleasure to greet a conference of working women. I will allow myself to pass over those subjects and questions that, of course, at the moment are the cause of the greatest concern to every working woman and to every politically conscious individual from among the working people; these are the most urgent questions— that of bread and that of the war situation. I know from the newspaper reports of your meetings that these questions have been dealt with exhaustively by Comrade Trotsky as far as war questions are concerned and by Comrades Yakovleva and Svidersky as far as the bread question is concerned; please, therefore, allow me to pass over those questions.

I should like to say a few words about the general tasks facing the working women's movement in the Soviet Republic, those that are, in general, connected with the transition to socialism, and those that are of particular urgency at the present time. Comrades, the question of the position of women was raised by Soviet power from the very beginning. It seems to me that any workers' state in the course of transition to socialism is faced with a double task. The first part of that task is relatively simple and easy. It concerns those old laws that kept women in a position of inequality as compared to men.

Participants in all emancipation movements in Western Europe have long since, not for decades but for centuries, put forward the demand that obsolete laws be annulled and women and men be made equal by law, but none of the democratic European states, none of the advanced republics have succeeded in putting it into effect, because wherever there is capitalism, wherever there is private property in land and factories, wherever the power of capital is preserved, the men retain their privileges. It was possible to put it into effect in Russia only because the power of the workers has been established here since October 25, 1917. From the very onset Soviet power set out to be the power of the working people, hostile to all forms of exploitation. It set itself the task of doing away with the possibility of the exploitation of the working people by the landowners and capitalists, of doing away with the rule of capital. Soviet power has been trying to make it possible for the working people to organise their lives without private property in land, without privately-owned factories, without that private property that everywhere, throughout the world, even where there is complete political liberty, even in the most democratic republics, keeps the working people in a state of what is actually poverty, and wage-slavery, and women in a state of double slavery.

Soviet power, the power of the working people, in the first months of its existence effected a very definite revolution in legislation that concerns women. Nothing whatever is left in the Soviet Republic of those laws that put women in a subordinate position. I am speaking specifically of those laws that took advantage of the weaker position of women and put them in a position of inequality and often, even, in a humiliating position, i.e., the laws on divorce and on children born out of wedlock and on the right of a woman to summon the father of a child for maintenance.

It is particularly in this sphere that bourgeois legislation, even, it must be said, in the most advanced countries, takes advantage of the weaker position of women to humiliate them and give them a status of inequality. It is particularly in this sphere that Soviet power has left nothing whatever of the old, unjust laws that were intolerable for working people. We may now say proudly and without any exaggeration that apart from Soviet Russia there is not a country in the world where women enjoy full equality and where women are not placed in the humiliating position felt particularly in day-to-day family life. This was one of our first and most important tasks.

If you have occasion to come into contact with parties that are hostile to the Bolsheviks, if there should come into your hands newspapers published in Russian in the regions occupied by Kolchak or Denikin, or if you happen to talk to people who share the views of those newspapers, you may often hear from them the accusation that Soviet power has violated democracy.

We, the representatives of Soviet power, Bolshevik communists and supporters of Soviet power are often accused of violating democracy and proof of this is given by citing the fact that Soviet power dispersed the Constituent Assembly.[27] We usually answer this accusation as follows: that democracy and that Constituent Assembly which came into being when private property still existed on earth, when there was no equality between people, when the one who possessed his own capital was the boss and the others worked for him and were his wage slaves—that was a democracy on which we place no value. Such democracy concealed slavery even in the most advanced countries. We socialists are supporters of democracy only insofar as it eases the position of the working and oppressed people. Throughout the world socialism has set itself the task of combating every kind of exploitation of man by man. That democracy has real value for us which serves the exploited, the under-privileged. If those who do not work are disfranchised that would be real equality between people. Those who do not work should not eat.

In reply to these accusations we say that the question must be presented in this way—how is democracy implemented in various countries? We see that equality is proclaimed in all democratic republics but in the civil laws and in laws on the rights of women, those that concern their position in the family and on divorce, we see inequality and the humiliation of women at every step, and we say that this is a violation of democracy specifically in respect of the oppressed. Soviet power has implemented democracy to a greater degree than any of the other, most advanced countries because it has not left in its laws any trace of the inequality of women. Again I say that no other state and no other legislation has ever done for women a half of what Soviet power did in the first months of its existence.

Laws alone, of course, are not enough, and we are by no means content with mere decrees. In the sphere of legislation, however, we have done everything required of us to put women in a position of equality and we have every right to be proud of it. The position of women in Soviet Russia is now ideal as compared with their position in the most advanced states. We tell ourselves, however, that this is, of course, only the beginning.

Owing to her work in the house, the woman is still in a difficult position. To effect her complete emancipation and make her the equal of the man it is necessary for housework to be socialised and for women to participate in common productive labour. Then women will occupy the same position as men.

Here we are not, of course, speaking of making women the equal of men as far as productivity of labour, the quantity of labour, the length of the working day, labour conditions, etc., are concerned; we mean that the woman should not, unlike the man, be oppressed because of her economic position. You all know that even when women have full rights, they still remain downtrodden because all housework is left to them. In most cases housework is the most unproductive, the most savage and the most arduous work a woman can do. It is exceptionally petty and does not include anything that would in any way promote the development of the woman.

In pursuance of the socialist ideal we want to struggle for the full implementation of socialism, and here an extensive field of labour opens up before women. We are now making serious preparations to clear the ground for the building of socialism, but the building of socialism will begin only when we have achieved the complete equality of women and undertake the new work together with women who have been emancipated from that petty, stultifying, unproductive work. This is a job that will take us many, many years.

This work cannot show any rapid results and will not produce a scintillating effect.

We are setting up model institutions, dining rooms and

nurseries, that will emancipate women from housework. And the work of organising all these institutions will fall mainly to women. It has to be admitted that in Russia today there are very few institutions that would help woman out of her state of household slavery. There is an insignificant number of them, and the conditions now obtaining in the Soviet Republic—the war and the food situation about which comrades have already given you the details—hinder us in this work. Still, it must be said that these institutions that liberate women from their position as household slaves are springing up wherever it is in any way possible.

We say that the emancipation of the workers must be effected by the workers themselves, and in exactly the same way the emancipation of working women is a matter for the working women themselves. The working women must themselves see to it that such institutions are developed, and this activity will bring about a complete change in their position as compared with what it was under the old, capitalist society.

In order to be active in politics under the old, capitalist regime special training was required, so that women played an insignificant part in politics, even in the most advanced and free capitalist countries. Our task is to make politics available to every working woman. Ever since private property in land and factories has been abolished and the power of the landowners and capitalists overthrown, the tasks of politics have become simple, clear and comprehensible to the working people as a whole, and to working women as well. In capitalist society the women's position is marked by such inequality that her participation in politics is only an insignificant fraction of man's participation. The power of the working people is necessary for a change to be wrought in this situation, for then the main tasks of politics will consist of matters directly affecting the fate of the working people themselves.

Here, too, the participation of working women is essential —not only of Party members and politically conscious women, but also of the non-party women and those who are least politically conscious. Here Soviet power opens up a wide field of activity to working women.

We have had a difficult time in the struggle against the forces hostile to Soviet Russia that have attacked her. It was difficult for us to fight on the battlefield against those forces who went to war against the power of the working people and in the field of food supplies against the profiteers, because the number of people, the number of working people, who came whole-heartedly to our aid with their own labour was much too small. Here, too, there is nothing Soviet power can appreciate as much as the help given by masses of non-party working women. They may know that in the old bourgeois society, perhaps, a complicated training was necessary for participation in politics and that this was not available to women. The political activity of the Soviet Republic is mainly the struggle against the landowners and capitalists, the struggle for the elimination of exploitation; political activity, therefore, is made available to the working woman in the Soviet Republic and it will consist in the working woman using her organisational ability to help the working man.

What we need is not only organisational work on a scale involving millions; we need organisational work on the smallest scale and this makes it possible for women to work as well. Women can work under war conditions when it is a question of helping the army or carrying on agitation in the army. Women should take an active part in all this so that the Red Army sees that it is being looked after, that solicitude is being displayed. Women can also work in the sphere of food distribution, on the improvement of public catering and everywhere opening dining rooms like those that are so numerous in Petrograd.

It is in these fields that the activities of working women acquire the greatest organisational significance. The participation of working women is also essential in the organisation and running of big experimental farms which should not be a task for individuals. This is something that cannot be carried out without the participation of a large number of working women. Working women will be very useful in this field in supervising the distribution of food and in making food products more easily obtainable. This work can well be done by non-party working women and its accomplishment will do more than anything else to strengthen socialist society.

We have abolished private property in land and almost completely abolished the private ownership of factories; Soviet power is now trying to ensure that all working people, non-Party as well as Party members, women as well as men, should take part in this economic development. The work that Soviet power has begun can only make progress when, instead of a few hundreds, millions and millions of women throughout Russia take part in it. We are sure that the cause of socialist development will then become sound. Then the working people will show that they can live and run their country without the aid of the landowners and capitalists. Then socialist construction will be so soundly based in Russia that no external enemies in other countries and none inside Russia will be any danger to the Soviet Republic.

Pravda No. 213,   *Collected Works*, Vol. 30
September 25, 1919

Soviet Power
and the Status of Women

The second anniversary of Soviet power is an occasion for taking stock of what has been done during this period and for reflecting on the significance and the aims of the revolution that has been accomplished.

The bourgeoisie and its supporters charge us with having violated democracy. We, on the other hand, assert that the Soviet revolution has given an unprecedented impulse to the development of democracy in breadth and in depth, democracy, that is, for the working people oppressed by capitalism, democracy for the overwhelming majority of the people, socialist democracy (for the working people), as distinct from bourgeois democracy (for the exploiters, for the capitalists, for the rich).

Who is right?

To give proper thought to this question and achieve a deeper understanding of it one must take stock of the experience of these two years and make better preparations for its further development.

The status of women makes clear in the most striking fashion the difference between bourgeois and socialist democracy and furnishes a most effective reply to the question posed.

In a bourgeois republic (i.e., where there is private ownership of land, factories, shares, etc.), be it the most democratic republic, women have never had equal rights, *anywhere in the world, in any one of the more advanced countries*. And this despite the fact that more than 125

73

years have passed since the French (bourgeois-democratic) Revolution.

In words bourgeois democracy promises equality and freedom, but in practice *not a single* bourgeois republic, even the more advanced, has granted women (half the human race) and men complete equality in the eyes of the law, or delivered women from dependence on and the oppression of the male.

Bourgeois democracy is the democracy of pompous phrases, solemn words, lavish promises and high-sounding slogans about *freedom and equality*, but in practice all this cloaks the lack of freedom and the inequality of women, the lack of freedom and the inequality for the working and exploited people.

Soviet or socialist democracy sweeps away these pompous but false words and declares ruthless war on the hypocrisy of "democrats", landowners, capitalists and farmers with bursting bins who are piling up wealth by selling surplus grain to the starving workers at speculation prices.

Down with this foul lie! There is no "equality", nor can there be, of oppressed and oppressor, exploited and exploiter. There is no real "freedom", nor can there be, so long as women are handicapped by men's legal privileges, so long as there is no freedom for the worker from the yoke of capital, no freedom for the labouring peasant from the yoke of the capitalist, landowner and merchant.

Let the liars and the hypocrites, the obtuse and the blind, the bourgeois and their supporters, deceive the people with talk about freedom in general, about equality in general and about democracy in general. We say to the workers and peasants—tear the mask from these liars, open the eyes of the blind. Ask them:

Is there equality of the two sexes?

Which nation is the equal of which?

Which *class* is the equal of which?

Freedom from what yoke or from the yoke of which class? Freedom for which class?

He who speaks about politics, democracy and freedom, about equality, about socialism, *without posing* these questions, without giving them priority, who does not fight against hushing them up, concealing and blunting them, is the worst enemy of the working people, a wolf in sheep's clothing, the rabid opponent of the workers and peasants, a lackey of the landowners, the tsars and the capitalists.

In the course of two years of Soviet power in one of the most backward countries of Europe more has been done to emancipate woman, to make her the equal of the "strong" sex, than has been done during the past 130 years by all the advanced, enlightened, "democratic" republics of the world taken together.

Education, culture, civilisation, freedom—all these high-sounding words are accompanied in all the capitalist, bourgeois republics of the world by incredibly foul, disgustingly vile, bestially crude laws that make women unequal in marriage and divorce, that make the child born out of wedlock and the "legally born" child unequal, and that give privileges to the male, and humiliate and degrade womankind.

The yoke of capital, the oppression of "sacred private property", the despotism of philistine obtuseness, the avarice of the small property-owner—these are the things that have prevented the most democratic bourgeois republics from abolishing these foul and filthy laws.

The Soviet Republic, the republic of workers and peasants, wiped out these laws at one stroke and did not leave standing a single stone of the edifice of bourgeois lies and bourgeois hypocrisy.

Down with this lie! Down with the liars who speak about freedom and equality *for all*, while there is an oppressed sex, oppressing classes, private ownership of capital and shares and people with bursting bins who use their surplus grain to enslave the hungry. Instead of freedom for all, instead of equality for all, let there be *struggle* against the oppressors and exploiters, *let the opportunity* to oppress and exploit be abolished. That is our slogan !

Freedom and equality for the oppressed sex!

Freedom and equality for the workers and labouring peasants!

Struggle against the oppressors, struggle against the capitalists, struggle against the kulak profiteers!

This is our fighting slogan, this is our proletarian truth, the truth of the fight against capital, the truth that we hurl in the face of the world of capital with its honeyed, hypocritical and pompous phrases about freedom and equality *in general*, about freedom and equality *for all*.

And it is because we have laid bare this hypocrisy, because, with revolutionary vigour, we are ensuring freedom and full rights for the oppressed and working people, against the oppressors, against the capitalists, against the kulaks—precisely because of this Soviet rule has become so dear to the workers of the whole world.

It is because of this, the sympathies of the working masses, the sympathies of the oppressed and exploited in all countries of the world, are with us on this occasion of the second anniversary of Soviet rule.

Because of this, on the occasion of the second anniversary of Soviet rule, despite the famine and cold, despite all the suffering caused by the imperialists' invasion of the Russian Soviet Republic, we are fully convinced of the justness of our cause, firmly convinced of the inevitable victory of Soviet power on a world scale.

Pravda No. 249,
November 6, 1919

Collected Works, Vol. 30

To the Bureau of the Women's Congress in Petrograd Gubernia

Comrades, since I have no opportunity of attending your Congress I should like to send you in writing my greetings and my best wishes for success.

We are now happily ending the Civil War. The Soviet Republic is becoming stronger through its victories over the exploiters. The Soviet Republic can and must, from now on, concentrate its forces on a more important task, one that is nearer and dearer to us, to all working people—on a bloodless war, a war for victory over hunger, cold and economic chaos. In this bloodless war, women workers and peasants have an especially big role to play.

May the Women's Congress in Petrograd Gubernia help found, consolidate and organise an army of working women for this bloodless war, a war that should and will bring still greater victories to Soviet power.

With Communist greetings,

V. Ulyanov (Lenin)

January 10, 1920

Petrogradskaya Pravda No. 11,
January 16, 1920

Collected Works, Vol. 30

To the Working Women

Comrades, the elections to the Moscow Soviet show that the Communist Party is gaining ground among the working class.

Working women must take a bigger part in the elections. The Soviet government is the first and only government in the world to have completely abolished all the old, despicable bourgeois laws which placed women in a position of inferiority to men, which placed men in a privileged position, for example, in respect of marital rights and of children. The Soviet government, the government of the working people, is the first and only government in the world to have abolished all the privileges of men in property questions, privileges which the laws on marriage and the family in all bourgeois republics, even the most democratic, still preserve.

Wherever there are landowners, capitalists and merchants, women cannot be the equal of men even before the law.

Where there are no landowners, capitalists or merchants, and where the government of the working people is building a new life without these exploiters, men and women are equal before the law.

But that is not enough.

Equality before the law is not necessarily equality in fact. We want the working woman to be the equal of the working man not only before the law but in actual fact. For this working women must take an increasing part in the administration of socialised enterprises and in the administration of the state.

By taking part in administration, women will quickly learn and will catch up with the men.

Elect more working women to the Soviet, both Communist women and non-party women. As long as they are honest working women capable of performing their work sensibly and conscientiously, even if they are not members of the Party—elect them to the Moscow Soviet!

Send more working women to the Moscow Soviet! Let the Moscow proletariat show that it is prepared to do everything, and is doing everything, to fight for victory, to fight the old inequality, the old bourgeois humiliation of women!

The proletariat cannot achieve complete liberty until it has won complete liberty for women.

February 21, 1920

N. Lenin

Pravda No. 40,
February 22, 1920

Collected Works, Vol. 30

On International Working Women's Day[28]

Capitalism combines formal equality with economic and, consequently, social inequality. That is one of the principal features of capitalism, one that is deliberately obscured by the supporters of the bourgeoisie, the liberals, and is not understood by petty-bourgeois democrats. This feature of capitalism, incidentally, renders it necessary for us in our resolute fight for economic equality openly to admit capitalist inequality, and even, under certain conditions, to make this open admission of inequality the basis of the proletarian statehood (the Soviet Constitution).

But even in the matter of formal equality (equality before the law, the "equality" of the well-fed and the hungry man, of the man of property and the propertyless), capitalism *cannot* be consistent. And one of the most glaring manifestations of this inconsistency is the *inequality* of women and men. Complete equality has not been granted even by the most progressive republican and democratic bourgeois states.

The Soviet Republic of Russia, on the other hand, at once swept away *all* legislative traces of the inequality of women *without exception*, and immediately ensured their complete equality before the law.

It is said that the best criterion of the cultural level is the legal status of women. This aphorism contains a grain of profound truth. In this respect only the dictatorship of the proletariat, only the socialist state could attain, and has attained, the highest cultural level.

The new, mighty and unparalleled upsurge in the working women's movement is therefore inevitably associated with the foundation (and consolidation) of the first Soviet Republic—and, in addition to and in connection with this, with the Communist International.[29]

Since mention has been made of those who were oppressed by capitalism, directly or indirectly, in whole or in part, it must be said that the Soviet system, and only the Soviet system, guarantees democracy. This is clearly shown by the position of the working class and the poor peasants. It is clearly shown by the position of women.

But the Soviet system is the last decisive struggle for the *abolition of classes*, for economic and social equality. Democracy, even democracy for those who were oppressed by capitalism, including the oppressed sex, *is not enough for us*.

The chief task of the working women's movement is to fight for economic and social equality, and not only formal equality, for women. The chief thing is to get women to take part in socially productive labour, to liberate them from "domestic slavery", to free them from their stupefying and humiliating subjugation to the eternal drudgery of the kitchen and the nursery.

This struggle will be a long one, and it demands a radical reconstruction both of social technique and of morals. But it will end in the complete triumph of communism.

March 4, 1920

Supplement to *Pravda* No. 52, March 7, 1920

Collected Works, Vol. 30

Greetings
to the All-Russia Conference
of Gubernia Soviet Women's Departments

**To the Presidium
of the All-Russia Conference
of Managers
of Gubernia Soviet Women's Departments
December 6, 1920**

Comrades, I deeply regret not having been able to attend your congress. Please convey my sincere greetings and best wishes for success to all men and women participating.

The participation of women in Party and government work is acquiring tremendous significance now that the war is over and peacetime organisational work has—and for a long time I hope—been brought into the foreground. In this work women must, and of course, will play the leading role.

V. Ulyanov (Lenin)
Chairman, Council of People's Commissars

Pravda No. 286,
December 19, 1920

Collected Works, Vol. 31

International Working Women's Day

The gist of Bolshevism and the Russian October Revolution is getting into politics the very people who were most oppressed under capitalism. They were downtrodden, cheated and robbed by the capitalists, both under the monarchy and in the bourgeois democratic republics. So long as the land and the factories were privately owned this oppression and deceit and the plunder of the people's labour by the capitalists were inevitable.

The essence of Bolshevism and the Soviet power is to expose the falsehood and mummery of bourgeois democracy, to abolish the private ownership of land and the factories and concentrate all state power in the hands of the working and exploited masses. They, these masses, get hold of politics, that is, of the business of building the new society. This is no easy task: the masses are downtrodden and oppressed by capitalism, but there is no other way—and there can be no other way—out of the wage slavery and bondage of capitalism.

But you cannot draw the masses into politics without drawing the women into politics as well. For the female half of the human race is doubly oppressed under capitalism. The working woman and the peasant woman are oppressed by capital, but over and above that, even in the most democratic of the bourgeois republics, they remain, firstly, deprived of some rights because the law does not give them equality with men; and secondly—and this is the main thing—they remain in "household bondage", they continue to be "household slaves", for they are overburdened with the drudgery of the most squalid and back-breaking and stultifying toil in the kitchen and the individual family household.

No party or revolution in the world has ever dreamed of striking so deep at the roots of the oppression and inequality of women as the Soviet, Bolshevik revolution is doing. Over here, in Soviet Russia, no trace is left of any inequality between men and women under the law. The Soviet power has eliminated all there was of the especially disgusting, base and hypocritical inequality in the laws on marriage and the family and inequality in respect of children.

This is only the first step in the liberation of woman. But none of the bourgeois republics, including the most democratic of them, has dared to take even this first step. The reason is awe of "sacrosanct private property".

The second and most important step is the abolition of the private ownership of land and the factories. This and this alone opens up the way towards a complete and actual emancipation of woman, her liberation from "household slavery" through the transition from petty individual housekeeping to a large-scale socialised domestic services.

This transition is a difficult one, because it involves the remoulding of the most deep-rooted, inveterate, hidebound and rigid "order" (indecency and barbarity, would be nearer the truth). But the transition has been started, the thing has been set in motion, we have taken the new path.

And so on this international working women's day countless meetings of working women in all countries of the world will send greetings to Soviet Russia, which first tackled this unparalleled and incredibly hard but great task, a task that is universally great and truly liberatory. There will be bracing calls not to lose heart in face of the fierce and frequently savage bourgeois reaction. The "freer" or "more democratic" a bourgeois country is, the wilder the rampage of its gang of capitalists against the workers' revolution, an example of this being the democratic republic of the United States of North America. But the mass of workers have already awakened. The dormant, somnolent and inert masses in America, Europe and even in backward Asia were finally roused by the imperialist war.

The ice has been broken in every corner of the world.

Nothing can stop the tide of the peoples' liberation from the imperialist yoke and the liberation of working men and women from the yoke of capital. This cause is being carried forward by tens and hundreds of millions of working men and women in town and countryside. That is why this cause of labour's freedom from the yoke of capital will triumph all over the world.

March 4, 1921

Published on March **8, 1921,**
in the supplement
to *Pravda* No. 51

Collected Works, Vol. 32

**Message of
Greetings to the Conference
of Representatives
of Women's Departments
of the Peoples of Soviet Regions
and Republics in the East**[30]

I deeply regret that I am unable to attend your conference because of the pressure of work. Please accept my heartfelt greetings and best wishes of success, especially in preparing for the forthcoming First All-Russia Non-Party Congress of Women of the East, which, correctly prepared and conducted, must greatly help *the cause of awakening the women of the East and uniting them organisationally.*

Lenin

Pravda No. 77,
April 10, 1921

Collected Works, Vol. 32

FROM The Fourth Anniversary
of the October Revolution

What were the chief manifestations, survivals, remnants of serfdom in Russia up to 1917? The monarchy, the system of social estates, landed proprietorship and land tenure, the inferior status of women, religion, and national oppression. Take any one of these Augean stables, which, incidentally, were left largely uncleansed by all the more advanced states when they accomplished *their* bourgeois-democratic revolutions one hundred and twenty-five, two hundred and fifty and more years ago (1649 in England); take any of these Augean stables, and you will see that we have cleansed them thoroughly. In a matter of *ten weeks*, from October 25 (November 7), 1917, to the dissolution of the Constituent Assembly (January 5, 1918), we accomplished a thousand times more in this respect than was accomplished by the bourgeois democrats and liberals (the Cadets) and by the petty-bourgeois democrats (the Mensheviks and the Socialist-Revolutionaries) *during the eight months* they were in power.

Those poltroons, gas-bags, vainglorious Narcissuses and petty Hamlets brandished their wooden swords—but did not even destroy the monarchy! We cleansed out all that monarchist muck as nobody had ever done before. We left not a stone of that ancient edifice standing, the social-estate system (even the most advanced countries, such as Britain, France and Germany, have not completely eliminated the survivals of this system to this day!). We have torn out the deep-seated roots of the social-estate system, namely, the remnants of feudalism and serfdom in the system of landownership, to the last. "One may argue" (there are plenty of quill-drivers, Cadets, Mensheviks and Socialist-Revolutionaries abroad to indulge in such arguments) as to what "in the long run" will be the outcome of the agrarian reform effected by the Great October Revolution. We have no desire at the moment to waste time on such controversies, for we are deciding this, as well as the mass of controversies connected with it, by struggle. But the fact cannot be denied that the petty-bourgeois democrats "compromised" with the landowners, the custodians of the traditions of serfdom, for eight months, while we completely swept the landowners and all their traditions from Russian soil in a few weeks.

Take religion, or the denial of rights to women, or the oppression and inequality of the non-Russian nationalities. These are all problems of the bourgeois-democratic revolution. The vulgar petty-bourgeois democrats talked about them for eight months. Not in a *single* one of the most advanced countries in the world have *these* questions been *completely* settled on *bourgeois-democratic* lines. In our country they have been settled completely by the legislation of the October Revolution. We have fought and are fighting religion in earnest. We have granted *all* the non-Russian nationalities *their own* republics or autonomous regions. We in Russia no longer have the base, mean and infamous denial of rights to women or inequality of the sexes, that disgusting survival of feudalism and medievalism which is being renovated by the avaricious bourgeoisie and the dull-witted and frightened petty bourgeoisie in every other country in the world without exception.

All this goes into the content of the bourgeois-democratic revolution. A hundred and fifty and two hundred and fifty years ago the progressive leaders of that revolution (or of those revolutions, if we consider each national variety of the one general type) promised to rid mankind of medieval privileges, of sex inequality, of privileged state religions (or "the idea of religion", or "religiosity" in general) and of national inequality. They promised, but did not keep their promises. They could not keep them, for they were hindered by their "respect"—for the "sacred private property". Our proletarian revolution was not afflicted with this accursed "respect" for this thrice-accursed medievalism and for the "sacred private property".

October 14, 1921

Pravda No. 234,
October 18, 1921

Collected Works, Vol. 33

FROM On the Significance
of Militant Materialism

In conclusion, I will cite an example which has nothing to do with philosophy, but does at any rate concern social questions, to which *Pod Znamenem Marxizma*[31] also desires to devote attention.

It is an example of the way in which modern pseudo-science serves in effect as a vehicle for the grossest and most infamous reactionary views.

I was recently sent a copy of *Ekonomist*[32] No. 1 (1922), published by the Eleventh Department of the Russian Technical Society. The young Communist who sent me this journal (he probably had no time to acquaint himself with its contents) rashly expressed an exceedingly sympathetic opinion of it. In reality the journal is—I do not know how deliberately—an organ of the modern feudalists, disguised of course under a cloak of science, democracy and so forth.

A certain Mr. P. A. Sorokin publishes in this journal an extensive, so-called "sociological", inquiry on "The Influence of the War". This learned article abounds in learned references to the "sociological" works of the author and his numerous teachers and colleagues abroad. Here is an example of his learning.

On page 83, I read:

"For every 10,000 marriages in Petrograd there are now 92.2 divorces—a fantastic figure. Of every 100 annulled marriages, 51.1 had lasted less than one year, 11 per cent less than one month, 22 per cent less than two months, 41 per cent less than three to six months and only 26 per cent over six months. These figures show that modern legal marriage is a form which conceals what is in effect extra-conjugal sexual intercourse, enabling lovers of 'strawberries' to satisfy their appetites in a 'legal' way" (*Ekonomist* No. 1, p. 83).

Both this gentleman and the Russian Technical Society which publishes this journal and gives space to this kind of argument no doubt regard themselves as adherents of democracy and would consider it a great insult to be called what they are in fact, namely, feudalists, reactionaries, "diploma'd flunkeys of clericalism".

Even the slightest acquaintance with the legislation of bourgeois countries on marriage, divorce and children born out of wedlock, and with the actual state of affairs in this respect, is enough to show anyone interested in the subject that modern bourgeois democracy, even in all the most democratic bourgeois republics, exhibits a truly feudal attitude in this respect towards women and towards children born out of wedlock.

This, of course, does not prevent the Mensheviks, the Socialist-Revolutionaries, a part of the anarchists and all the similar parties in the West from shouting about democracy and how it is being violated by the Bolsheviks. But as a matter of fact the Bolshevik revolution is the only consistently democratic revolution in respect to such questions as marriage, divorce and the position of children born out of wedlock. And this is a question which in a most direct manner affects the interests of more than half the population of any country. The Bolshevik revolution, in spite of the vast number of bourgeois revolutions which preceded it and which called themselves democratic, was the first and only revolution to wage a resolute struggle in this respect both against reaction and feudalism and against the usual hypocrisy of the ruling and propertied classes.

If 92 divorces for every 10,000 marriages seem to Mr. Sorokin a fantastic figure, one can only suppose that either the author lived and was brought up in a monastery so entirely walled-off from life that hardly anyone will believe such a monastery ever existed, or that he is distorting the truth in the interest of reaction and the bourgeoisie. Anybody who has some slight acquaintance with social conditions in bourgeois countries knows that the real number of actual divorces (of course, not sanctioned by church and law) is everywhere immeasurably greater.

The only difference between Russia and other countries in this respect is that our laws do not sanctify hypocrisy and the debasement of the woman and her child, but openly and in the name of the government declare systematic war on all hypocrisy and all debasement.

The Marxist magazine will have to wage war also on these modern "educated" feudalists. Not a few of them, very likely, are in receipt of government money and are employed by our government to educate our youth, although they are no more fitted for this than notorious perverters are fitted for the post of superintendents of educational establishments for the young.

The working class of Russia has succeeded in winning power; but it has not yet learned to utilise it, for otherwise it would have long ago very politely dispatched such teachers and members of learned societies to countries with a bourgeois "democracy". That is the proper place for such feudalists.

But it will learn, given the will to learn.

March 12, 1922

Pod Znamenem Marxizma No. 3,   *Collected Works*, Vol. 33
March 1922

To the Non-Party Conference of Factory and Peasant Women of Moscow City and Moscow Gubernia[33]

Dear Comrades,

My best thanks for your kind wishes and greetings. I am very sorry that I am unable to attend in person. Congratulations on the occasion of the Fifth Anniversary of the Revolution and all best wishes for the success of your meeting.

Yours,
Lenin

November 6, 1922
Published in November 1922

CLARA ZETKIN

My Recollections of Lenin

(An Interview on the Woman Question)

From My Memorandum Book

Comrade Lenin repeatedly discussed with me the problem of women's rights. He obviously attached great importance to the women's movement, which was to him an essential component of the mass movement that in certain circumstances might become decisive. Needless to say he saw full social equality of women as a principle which no Communist could dispute.

We had our first lengthy talk on this subject in the autumn of 1920, in Lenin's big study in the Kremlin. Lenin sat at his desk, which was covered with books and papers, indicating study and work without the "brilliant disorder" associated with genius.

"We must by all means set up a powerful international women's movement on a clear-cut theoretical basis," he began after greeting me. "It is clear that without Marxist theory we cannot have proper practice. Here, too, we Communists need the greatest clarity of principle. We must draw a sharp line between us and all other parties. Our Second International Congress[34] unfortunately did not come up to expectations in discussing the question of women. It posed the question but did not get around to taking a definite stand. A committee is still in charge of the matter. It is to draft a resolution, theses and directives but has made little progress so far. You must help it."

I had already heard from others what Lenin was now telling me and I expressed my amazement. I was full of enthusiasm for everything Russian women had done during the revolution and what they were doing now for its defence and further development. As for the standing

97

and activity of women in the Bolshevik Party, I thought that it was a model party—indeed, *the* model party. It alone supplied the international Communist women's movement with a valuable trained and experienced force and set a great example for history.

"That is true, it's wonderful," Lenin remarked with a faint smile. "In Petrograd, here in Moscow, and in other cities and industrial centres, proletarian women showed up splendidly during the revolution. We would not have won without them, or hardly. That is my opinion. What courage they showed and how courageous they still are! Imagine the suffering and privation they are enduring. But they are holding out because they want to defend the Soviets, because they want freedom and communism. Yes, our working women are magnificent class fighters. They are worthy of admiration and love. In general, it must be acknowledged that even the ladies of the 'Constitutional Democrats' in Petrograd showed greater courage in fighting us than those wretched military Cadets.[35]

"It's true that we have reliable, intelligent and tireless women in our Party. They hold important posts in the Soviets, Executive Committees, People's Commissariats, and public offices of every kind. Many of them work day and night either in the Party or among the workers and peasants or in the Red Army. That is of great value to us. It is important for women all over the world, as it is evidence of the capacity of women, of the great value of the work they do for society. The first proletarian dictatorship is truly paving the way for the complete social equality of women. It eradicates more prejudice than volumes of feminist literature. However, in spite of all this, we do not yet have an international Communist women's movement and we must have one without fail. We must immediately set about starting it. Without such a movement, the work of our International and of its parties is incomplete and never will be complete. Yet our revolutionary work has to be fulfilled in its entirety. Tell me how Communist work is getting on abroad."

I did—as well as I could at the time, with the links between the Comintern parties still very loose and irregular. Lenin listened attentively, leaning slightly forward, with no sign of boredom, impatience or fatigue, keenly following even details of secondary importance. I have never known anyone who was a better listener or who could co-ordinate and generalise all that he had heard as fast as he did. That was evident from the short and always very specific questions he asked from time to time about what I told him, and from the fact that he returned to this or that particular of my narrative later on. Lenin made some brief notes.

Naturally, I spoke in great detail about the state of affairs in Germany. I told Lenin of the vast importance which Rosa Luxemburg attached to drawing the greatest number of women into the revolutionary struggle. When the Communist Party had been founded, she insisted that a women's newspaper be published. When Leo Jogiches and I met for the last time—thirty-six hours before he was murdered—he discussed the Party's plan of work with me. He gave me various tasks to perform, among them a plan for the organisation of work among working women. The Party tackled this question at its first illegal conference. The trained and experienced women agitators and leaders who had become prominent before and during the war had almost without exception remained Social-Democrats of the one or the other shade, and kept the agitated and active proletarian women under their sway. However, there was already a small nucleus of energetic, devoted women who took part in the Party's every job and every battle. Furthermore, the Party itself had already organised methodical activity among the working women. Of course all this was merely a start, but a good start nevertheless.

"Not bad, not bad at all," Lenin said. "The Communist women's energy, devotion and enthusiasm, their courage and intelligence during the illegal and semi-legal periods, promise well for the development of our work. It would be useful for the expansion of the Party and the growth of its strength to win over the masses and carry through actions. But how about giving all the comrades a clear understanding of the fundamentals of this question and training them—how are you getting along in this respect? This is what counts most in the work among the masses. It is very important in terms of the ideas we convey to the masses, and of the things we want the masses to adopt and take inspiration from. I cannot remember at the moment who said 'It takes inspiration to do great deeds'. We and the working people of the whole world still have really great deeds to perform. What inspires your comrades, the proletarian women of Germany? What about their proletarian class-consciousness? Do their interests and activities centre on the political demands of the moment? What is the focal point of their thoughts?

"I have heard strange things about that from Russian and German comrades. I must tell you what I mean. I understand that in Hamburg a gifted Communist woman is bringing out a newspaper for prostitutes, and is trying to organise them for the revolutionary struggle. Now Rosa, a true Communist, felt and acted like a human being when she wrote an article in defence of prostitutes who have landed in jail for violating a police regulation concerning their sad trade. They are unfortunate double victims of bourgeois society. Victims, first, of its accursed system of property and, secondly, of its accursed moral hypocrisy. There's no doubt about this. Only a coarse-grained and short-sighted person could forget this. To understand this is one thing, but it is quite another thing—how shall I put it?—to organise the prostitutes as a special revolutionary guild contingent and publish a trade union paper for them. Are there really no industrial working women left in Germany who need organising, who need a newspaper, who should be enlisted in your struggle? This is a morbid deviation. It strongly reminds me of the literary vogue which made a sweet madonna out of every prostitute. Its origin was sound too: social sympathy, and indignation against the moral hypocrisy of the honourable bourgeoisie. But the healthy principle underwent bourgeois corrosion and degenerated. The question of prostitution will confront us even in our country with many a difficult problem. Return the prostitute to productive work, find her a place in the social economy—that is the thing to do. But the present state of our economy and all the other circumstances make it a difficult and complicated matter. Here you have an aspect of the woman problem which faces us in all its magnitude, after the proletariat has come to power, and demands a practical solution. It will still require a great deal of effort here in Soviet Russia. But to return to your special problem in Germany. Under no circumstances should the Party look calmly upon such improper acts of its members. It causes confusion and splits our forces. Now what have *you* done to stop it?"

Before I could answer Lenin continued:

"The record of your sins, Clara, is even worse. I have been told that at the evenings arranged for reading and discussion with working women, sex and marriage problems come first. They are said to be the main objects of interest in your political instruction and educational work. I could not believe my ears when I heard that. The first state of proletarian dictatorship is battling with the counter-revolutionaries of the whole world. The situation in Germany itself calls for the greatest unity of all proletarian revolutionary forces, so that they can repel the counter-revolution which is pushing on. But active Communist women are busy discussing sex problems and the forms of marriage—'past, present and future'. They consider it their most important task to enlighten working women on these questions. It is said that a pamphlet on the sex question written by a Communist authoress from Vienna enjoys the greatest popularity. What rot that booklet is! The workers read what is right in it long ago in Bebel. Only not in the tedious, cut-and-dried form found in the pamphlet but in the form of gripping agitation that strikes out at bourgeois society. The mention of Freud's hypotheses is designed to give the pamphlet a scientific veneer, but it is so much bungling by an amateur. Freud's theory has now become a fad. I mistrust sex theories expounded in articles, treatises, pamphlets, etc.—in short, the theories dealt with in that specific literature which sprouts so luxuriantly on the dung heap of bourgeois society. I mistrust those who are always absorbed in the sex problems, the way an Indian saint is absorbed in the contemplation of his navel. It seems to me that this super-abundance of sex theories, which for the most part are mere hypotheses, and often quite arbitrary ones, stems from a personal need. It springs from the desire to justify one's own abnormal or excessive sex life before bourgeois morality and to plead for tolerance towards oneself. This veiled respect for bourgeois morality is as repugnant to me as rooting about in all that bears on sex. No matter how rebellious and revolutionary it may be made to appear, it is in the final analysis thoroughly bourgeois. Intellectuals and others like them are particularly keen on this. There is no room for it in the Party, among the class-conscious, fighting proletariat."

I interposed that where private property and the bourgeois social order prevail, questions of sex and marriage gave rise to manifold problems, conflicts and suffering for women of all social classes and strata. As far as women are concerned, the war and its consequences exacerbated the existing conflicts and suffering to the utmost precisely in the sphere of sexual relations. Problems formerly concealed from women were now laid bare. To this was added the atmosphere of incipient revolution. The world of old emotions and thoughts was cracking up. Former social connections were loosening and breaking. The makings of new relations between people were appearing. Interest in the relevant problems was an expression of the need for enlightenment and a new orientation. It was also a reaction against the distortions and hypocrisy of bourgeois society. Knowledge of the modifications of the forms of marriage and family that took place in the course of history, and of their dependence on economics, would serve to rid the minds of working women of their preconceived idea of the eternity of bourgeois society. The critically historical attitude to this had to lead to an unrelenting analysis of bourgeois society, an exposure of its essence and its consequences, including the branding of false sex morality. All roads led to Rome. Every truly Marxist analysis of an important part of the ideological superstructure of society, of an outstanding social phenomenon, had to lead to an analysis of bourgeois society and its foundation, private property. It should lead to the conclusion that "Carthage must be destroyed".

Lenin nodded with a smile.

"There you are! You defend your comrades and your Party like a lawyer. What you say is of course true. But that can at best excuse, not justify, the mistake made in Germany. It remains a mistake. Can you assure me in all sincerity that during those reading and discussion evenings, questions of sex and marriage are dealt with from the point of view of mature, vital historical materialism? This presupposes wide-ranging, profound knowledge, and the fullest Marxist mastery of a vast amount of material. Do you now have the forces you need for that? Had you had them, a pamphlet like the one we spoke about would not have been used for instruction during reading and discussion evenings. It is being recommended and disseminated instead of being criticised. Why is the approach to this problem inadequate and un-Marxist? Because sex and marriage problems are not treated as only part of the main social problem. Conversely, the main social problem is presented as a part, an appendage to the sex problem. The important point recedes into the background. Thus not only is this question obscured, but also thought, and the class-consciousness of working women in general, is dulled.

"Besides, and this isn't the least important point, Solomon the Wise said there is a time for everything. I ask you, is this the time to keep working women busy for months at a stretch with such questions as how to love or be loved, how to woo or be wooed? This, of course, with regard to the 'past, present and future', and among the various races. And it is proudly styled historical materialism. Nowadays all the thoughts of Communist women, of working women, should be centred on the proletarian revolution, which will lay the foundation, among other things, for the necessary revision of material and sexual relations. Just now we must really give priority to problems other than the forms of marriage prevalent among Australia's aborigines, or marriage between brother and sister in ancient times. For the German proletariat, the problem of the Soviets, of the Versailles Treaty[36] and its impact on the lives of women, the problem of unemployment, of falling wages, of taxes and many other things remain the order of the day. To be brief, I am still of the opinion that this sort of political and social education of working women is wrong, absolutely wrong. How could you keep quiet about it? You should have set your authority against it."

I told my fervent friend that I had never failed to criticise and to remonstrate with the leading women comrades in various places. But, as he knew, no prophet is honoured in his own country or in his own house. By my criticism I had drawn upon myself the suspicion that "survivals of a Social-Democratic attitude and old-fashioned philistinism were still strong" in my mind. However, in the end my criticism had proved effective. Sex and marriage were no longer the focal point in lectures at discussion evenings. Lenin resumed the thread of his argument.

"Yes, yes, I know that," he said. "Many people rather suspect *me* of philistinism on this account, although such an attitude is repugnant to me—it conceals so much narrow-mindedness and hypocrisy. Well, I'm unruffled by it. Yellow-beaked fledgelings newly hatched from their bourgeois-tainted eggs are all so terribly clever. We have to put up with that without mending our ways. The youth movement is also affected with the modern approach to the sex problem and with excessive interest in it."

Lenin emphasised the word "modern" with an ironical, deprecating gesture.

"I was also told that sex problems are a favourite subject in your youth organisations too, and that there are hardly enough lecturers on this subject. This nonsense is especially dangerous and damaging to the youth movement. It can easily lead to sexual excesses, to overstimulation of sex life and to wasted health and strength of young people. You must fight that too. There is no lack of contact between the youth movement and the women's movement. Our Communist women everywhere should cooperate methodically with young people. This will be a continuation of motherhood, will elevate it and extend it from the individual to the social sphere. Women's incipient social life and activities must be promoted, so that they can outgrow the narrowness of their philistine, individualistic psychology centred on home and family. But this is incidental.

"In our country, too, considerable numbers of young people are busy 'revising bourgeois conceptions and morals' in the sex question. And let me add that this involves a considerable section of our best boys and girls, of our truly promising youth. It is as you have just said. In the atmosphere created by the aftermath of war and by the revolution which has begun, old ideological values, finding themselves in a society whose economic foundations are undergoing a radical change, perish, and lose their restraining force. New values crystallise slowly, in the struggle. With regard to relations between people, and between man and woman, feelings and thoughts are also becoming revolutionised. New boundaries are being drawn between the rights of the individual and those of the community, and hence also the duties of the individual. Things are still in complete, chaotic ferment. The direction and potentiality of the various contradictory tendencies can still not be seen clearly enough. It is a slow and often very painful process of passing away and coming into being. All this applies also to the field of sexual relations, marriage, and the family. The decay, putrescence, and filth of bourgeois marriage with its difficult dissolution, its licence for the husband and bondage for the wife, and its disgustingly false sex morality and relations fill the best and most spiritually active of people with the utmost loathing.

"The coercion of bourgeois marriage and bourgeois legislation on the family enhance the evil and aggravate the conflicts. It is the coercion of 'sacrosanct' property. It sanctifies venality, baseness, and dirt. The conventional hypocrisy of 'respectable' bourgeois society takes care of the rest. People revolt against the prevailing abominations and perversions. And at a time when mighty nations are being destroyed, when the former power relations are being disrupted, when a whole social world is beginning to decline, the sensations of the individual undergo a rapid change. A stimulating thirst for different forms of enjoyment easily acquires an irresistible force. Sexual and marriage reforms in the bourgeois sense will not do. In the sphere of sexual relations and marriage, a revolution is approaching—in keeping with the proletarian revolution. Of course, women and young people are taking a deep interest in the complex tangle of problems which have arisen as a result of this. Both the former and the latter suffer greatly from the present messy state of sex relations. Young people rebel against them with the vehemence of their years. This is only natural. Nothing could be falser than to preach monastic self-denial and the sanctity of the filthy bourgeois morals to young people. However, it is hardly a good thing that sex, already strongly felt in the physical sense, should at such a time assume so much prominence in the psychology of young people. The consequences are nothing short of fatal. Ask Comrade Lilina about it. She ought to have had many experiences in her extensive work at educational institutions of various kinds and you know that she is a Communist through and through, and has no prejudices.

"Youth's altered attitude to questions of sex is of course 'fundamental', and based on theory. Many people call it 'revolutionary' and 'communist'. They sincerely believe that this is so. I am an old man, and I do not like it. I may be a morose ascetic, but quite often this so-called 'new sex life' of young people—and frequently of the adults too—seems to me purely bourgeois and simply an extension of the good old bourgeois brothel. All this has nothing in common with free love as we Communists understand it. No doubt you have heard about the famous theory that in communist society satisfying sexual desire and the craving for love is as simple and trivial as 'drinking a glass of water'. A section of our youth has gone mad, absolutely mad, over this 'glass-of-water theory'. It has been fatal to many a young boy and girl. Its devotees assert that it is a Marxist theory. I want no part of the kind of Marxism which infers all phenomena and all changes in the ideological superstructure of society directly and blandly from its economic basis, for things are not as simple as all that. A certain Frederick Engels has established this a long time ago with regard to historical materialism.

"I consider the famous 'glass-of-water' theory as completely un-Marxist and, moreover, as anti-social. It is not only what nature has given but also what has become culture, whether of a high or low level, that comes into play in sexual life. Engels pointed out in his *Origin of the Family* how significant it was that the common sexual relations had developed into individual sex love and thus became purer. The relations between the sexes are not simply the expression of a mutual influence between economics and a physical want deliberately singled out for physiological examination. It would be rationalism and not Marxism to attempt to refer the change in these relations directly to the economic basis of society in isolation from its connection with the ideology as a whole. To be sure, thirst has to be quenched. But would a normal person normally lie down in the gutter and drink from a puddle? Or even from a glass whose edge has been greased by many lips? But the social aspect is more important than anything else. The drinking of water is really an individual matter. But it takes two people to make love, and a third person, a new life, is likely to come into being. This deed has a social complexion and constitutes a duty to the community.

"As a Communist I have no liking at all for the 'glass-of-water' theory, despite its attractive label: 'emancipation of love.' Besides, emancipation of love is neither a novel nor a communistic idea. You will recall that it was advanced in fine literature around the middle of the past century as 'emancipation of the heart'. In bourgeois practice it materialised into emancipation of the flesh. It was preached with greater talent than now, though I cannot judge how it was practised. Not that I want my criticism to breed asceticism. That is farthest from my thoughts. Communism should not bring asceticism, but joy and strength, stemming, among other things, from a consummate love life. Whereas today, in my opinion, the obtaining plethora of sex life yields neither joy nor strength. On the contrary, it impairs them. This is bad, very bad, indeed, in the epoch of revolution.

"Young people are particularly in need of joy and strength. Healthy sports, such as gymnastics, swimming, hiking, physical exercises of every description and a wide range of intellectual interests is what they need, as well as learning, study and research, and as far as possible collectively. This will be far more useful to young people than endless lectures and discussions on sex problems and the so-called living by one's nature. *Mens sana in corpore sano*. Be neither monk nor Don Juan, but not anything in between either, like a German philistine. You know the young comrade X. He is a splendid lad, and highly gifted. For all that, I am afraid that he will never amount to anything. He has one love affair after another. This is not good for the political struggle and for the revolution. I will not vouch for the reliability or the endurance of women whose love affair is intertwined with politics, or for the men who run after every petticoat and let themselves in with every young female. No, no, that does not go well with revolution."

Lenin sprang to his feet, slapped the table with his hand and paced up and down the room.

"The revolution calls for concentration and rallying of every nerve by the masses and by the individual. It does not tolerate orgiastic conditions so common among d'Annunzio's decadent heroes and heroines. Promiscuity in sexual matters is bourgeois. It is a sign of degeneration. The proletariat is a rising class. It does not need an intoxicant to stupefy or stimulate it, neither the intoxicant of sexual laxity or of alcohol. It should and will not forget the vileness, the filth and the barbarity of capitalism. It derives its strongest inspiration to fight from its class position, from the communist ideal. What it needs is clarity, clarity, and more clarity. Therefore, I repeat, there must be no weakening, no waste and no dissipation of energy. Self-control and self-discipline are not slavery; not in matters of love either. But excuse me, Clara, I have strayed far from the point which we set out to discuss. Why have you not called me to order? Worry has set me talking. I take the future of our youth very close to heart. It is part and parcel of the revolution. Whenever harmful elements appear, which creep from bourgeois society to the world of the revolution and spread like the roots of prolific weeds, it is better to take action against them quickly. The questions we have dealt with are also part of the women's problems."

Lenin spoke with great animation and deep persuasion. I could feel that his every word came from the heart, and the expression on his face added to this feeling. From time to time he punctuated some idea with energetic gestures. I was astonished to see how much attention he devoted to trivial matters and how familiar he was with them, side by side with highly important political problems. And not only as concerned Soviet Russia, but also the still capitalist countries. Splendid Marxist that he was, he grasped the particular wherever and in whatever form it revealed itself, in its relation to, and its bearing upon, the whole. All his zest and purpose was concentrated with unshakeable singleness, like irresistible forces of nature, upon the one goal of speeding the revolution as a work of the masses. He evaluated everything in terms of its effect on the conscious motive forces of the revolution, both national and international, for while he evaluated the historically conditioned features of the individual countries and their different stages of development, he always had his eyes on the indivisible world-wide proletarian revolution.

"Comrade Lenin, how I regret," I exclaimed, "that your words have not been heard by hundreds and thousands of people. As you know, you do not have to convert me.

But how important it would be for friend and foe to hear your opinion!"

Lenin smiled amiably.

"I may speak or write some day on the questions we have discussed. But later, not now. Now all our time and strength must be concentrated on other things. There are bigger and more difficult jobs to do. The struggle to maintain and strengthen the Soviet state is not yet over by any means. We have to digest the outcome of the Polish War[37] and to make the most we can of it. Wrangel is still hanging on in the South. It is true, I am deeply convinced that we shall cope with him. That will give the British and French imperialists and their small vassals something to think about. But the most difficult part of our task, reconstruction, is still ahead. That will also bring the problems of sex relations, marriage and the family to the foreground. In the meantime, you will have to handle it as best you can where and when it is necessary. You should not allow these questions to be handled in an un-Marxist way or to serve as the basis for disruptive deviations and intrigues. Now at last I come to your work."

Lenin consulted his watch.

"Half of the time I have at my disposal for you," he said, "has already expired. I have chatted too long. You are to work out the leading theses on communist work among women. I know your principled approach and practical experience. So our talk about this will be brief; you had better get busy. What do you think the theses should be?"

I gave him a concise account on this score. Lenin nodded approvingly a few times without interrupting. When I was through I looked at him questioningly.

"Right," he remarked. "It would also be a good thing if you were to inform a meeting of responsible women Party comrades about it and to discuss it with them. Too bad Comrade Inessa* is not here. She is sick and has gone to the Caucasus. Put the theses in writing after the discussion. A committee will look them over and the Executive Committee will make the final decision. I give my opinion on only some of the main points, on which I fully share your views. They seem important to me also for our pre-

---

* I.e., Inessa Armand.—*Ed.*

sent agitation and propaganda work if it is to pave the way for action, for successful fighting.

"The theses must emphasise strongly that true emancipation of women is not possible except through communism. You must lay stress on the unbreakable connection between woman's human and social position and the private ownership of the means of production. This will draw a strong, ineradicable line against the bourgeois movement for the 'emancipation of women'. This will also give us a basis for examining the woman question as part of the social, working-class question, and to bind it firmly with the proletarian class struggle and the revolution. The communist women's movement itself must be a mass movement, a part of the general mass movements; and not only of the proletarians, but of all the exploited and oppressed, of all victims of capitalism or of the dominant class. Therein, too, lies the significance of the women's movement for the class struggle of the proletariat and its historic mission, the creation of a communist society. We can be legitimately proud that we have the flower of revolutionary womanhood in our Party, in the Comintern. But this is not decisive, we have to win over the millions of working women in town and country for our struggle and, particularly, for the communist reconstruction of society. There can be no real mass movement without the women.

"We derive our organisational ideas from our ideological conceptions. We want no separate organisations of communist women! She who is a Communist belongs as a member to the Party, just as he who is a Communist. They have the same rights and duties. There can be no difference of opinion on that score. However, we must not shut our eyes to the facts. The Party must have organs—working groups, commissions, committees, sections or whatever else they may be called—with the specific purpose of rousing the broad masses of women, bringing them into contact with the Party and keeping them under its influence. This naturally requires that we carry on systematic work among the women. We must teach the awakened women, win them over for the proletarian class struggle under the leadership of the Communist Party, and equip them for it. When I say this I have in mind not only proletarian women, whether they work in mills or cook the family meal. I also have in mind the peasant women and the women of the various sections of the lower middle class. They, too, are victims of capitalism, and more than ever since the war. The lack of interest in politics and the otherwise anti-social and backward psychology of these masses of women, the narrow scope of their activities and the whole pattern of their lives are undeniable facts. It would be silly to ignore them, absolutely silly. We must have our own groups to work among them, special methods of agitation, and special forms of organisation. This is not bourgeois 'feminism'; it is a practical revolutionary expediency."

I told Lenin that his arguments were a valuable encouragement for me. Many comrades, very good ones, too, vehemently opposed the Party's setting up special groups for planned work among women. They denounced it as a return to the notorious "emancipation of women" movement, to Social-Democratic traditions. They claimed that since the Communist Parties gave equality to women they should, consequently, carry on work without differentiation among all the working people in general. The approach to men and to women should be the same. Any attempt to consider the circumstances which Lenin had noted concerning agitation and organisation would be branded by the exponents of this view as opportunism, as renunciation and betrayal of fundamental principles.

"This is not new and not conclusive," Lenin said. "Do not let it mislead you. Why are there nowhere as many women in the Party as men, not even in Soviet Russia? Why is the number of women in the trade unions so small? These facts give one food for thought. Denial of the indispensable special groups for work among the masses of women is part of the very principled, very radical attitude of our dear friends of the Communist Workers' Party.[38] They are of the opinion that only one form of organisation should exist—a workers' union. I know about it. Principles are invoked by many revolutionary-minded but confused people whenever there is a lack of understanding, i.e., whenever the mind refuses to grasp the obvious facts that ought to be heeded. How do such guardians of the 'purity of principles' cope with the historical necessities of our revolutionary policy? All their talk collapses in face of the inexorable necessities. We cannot exercise the dictatorship of the proletariat without having millions of women on our side. Nor can we engage in communist construction without them. We must find a way to reach them. We must study and search in order to find this way.

"It is therefore perfectly right for us to put forward demands for the benefit of women. This is not a minimum programme, nor a programme of reform in the Social-Democratic sense, in the sense of the Second International.[39] It does not go to show that we believe the bourgeoisie and its state will last forever, or even for a long time. Nor is it an attempt to pacify the masses of women with reforms and to divert them from the path of revolutionary struggle. It is nothing of the sort, and not any sort of reformist humbug either. Our demands are no more than practical conclusions, drawn by us from the crying needs and disgraceful humiliations that weak and underprivileged woman must bear under the bourgeois system. We demonstrate thereby that we are aware of these needs and of the oppression of women, that we are conscious of the privileged position of the men, and that we hate—yes, hate—and want to remove whatever oppresses and harasses the working woman, the wife of the worker, the peasant woman, the wife of the little man, and even in many respects the woman of the propertied classes. The rights and social measures we demand of bourgeois society for women are proof that we understand the position and interests of women and that we will take note of them under the proletarian dictatorship. Naturally, not as soporific and patronising reformists. No, by no means. But as revolutionaries who call upon the women to take a hand as equals in the reconstruction of the economy and of the ideological superstructure."

I assured Lenin that I was of the same opinion, but that it would no doubt be opposed. Uncertain and timid minds would reject it as suspicious opportunism. Nor could it be denied that our present demands for women might be incorrectly understood and interpreted.

"What of it?" Lenin exclaimed, somewhat annoyed. "This risk exists in everything we say and do. If we are going to let fear of this stop us from doing the advisable and necessary, we might as well turn into Indian stylites. We mustn't budge, we mustn't budge on any account, or we shall tumble from the lofty pillar of our principles! In our case it is not only a matter of what we demand, but also of how we demand. I believe I have made that sufficiently clear. It stands to reason that in our propaganda we must not make a fetish out of our demands for women. No, we must fight now for these and now for other demands, depending on the existing conditions, and naturally always in association with the general interests of the proletariat.

"Every tussle of this kind sets us at loggerheads with the respectable bourgeois clique and its no less respectable reformist lackeys. This compels the latter either to fight under our leadership—which they do not want—or to drop their disguise. Thus, the struggle fences us off from them and shows our communist face. It wins us the confidence of the mass of women, who feel themselves exploited, enslaved and crushed by the domination of the man, by the power of their employers and by bourgeois society as a whole. Betrayed and abandoned by all, working women come to realise that they must fight together with us. Must I avow, or make you avow, that the struggle for women's rights must also be linked with our principal aim—the conquest of power and the establishment of the dictatorship of the proletariat? At present, this is, and will continue to be, our alpha and omega. That is clear, absolutely clear. But the broad masses of working women will not feel irresistibly drawn to the struggle for state power if we harp on just this one demand, even though we may blare it forth on the trumpets of Jericho. No, a thousand times no! We must combine our appeal politically in the minds of the female masses with the sufferings, the needs and the wishes of the working women. They should all know what the proletarian dictatorship will mean to them—complete equality of rights with men, both legal and in practice, in the family, the state and in society, and that it also spells the annihilation of the power of the bourgeoisie."

"Soviet Russia proves this," I exclaimed. "This will be our great example!"

Lenin went on:

"Soviet Russia casts a new light on our demands for women. Under the dictatorship of the proletariat they are no longer an object of struggle between the proletariat and the bourgeoisie. Once they are carried out, they serve as bricks for the building of communist society. This shows the women on the other side of the border the decisive importance of the conquest of power by the proletariat. The difference between their status here and there must be demonstrated in bold relief in order to win the support of the masses of women in the revolutionary class struggles of the proletariat. Mobilisation of the female masses, carried out with a clear understanding of principles and on a firm organisational basis, is a vital question for the Communist Parties and their victories. But let us not deceive ourselves. Our national sections still lack the proper understanding of this question. They adopt a passive, wait-and-see attitude when it comes to creating a mass movement of working women under communist leadership. They do not realise that developing and leading such a mass movement is an important part of all Party activity, as much as half of all the Party work. Their occasional recognition of the need and value of a purposeful, strong and numerous communist women's movement is but platonic lip-service rather than a steady concern and task of the Party.

"They regard agitation and propaganda among women and the task of rousing and revolutionising them as of secondary importance, as the job of just the women Communists. None but the latter are rebuked because the matter does not move ahead more quickly and strongly. This is wrong, fundamentally wrong! It is outright separatism. It is equality of women *à rebours*, as the French say, i.e., equality reversed. What is at the bottom of the incorrect attitude of our national sections? (I am not speaking of Soviet Russia.) In the final analysis, it is an underestimation of women and of their accomplishments. That's just what it is! Unfortunately, we may still say of many of our comrades, 'Scratch the Communist and a philistine appears.' To be sure, you have to scratch the sensitive spots,—such as their mentality regarding women. Could there be any more palpable proof than the common sight of a man calmly watching a woman wear herself out with trivial, monotonous, strength- and time-consuming work, such as her housework, and watching her spirit shrinking, her mind growing dull, her heartbeat growing faint, and her will growing slack? It goes without saying that I am not referring to the bourgeois ladies who dump all housework and the care for their children on the hired help. What I say applies to the vast majority of women, including the wives of workers, even if these spend the day at the factory and earn money.

"Very few husbands, not even the proletarians, think of how much they could lighten the burdens and worries of their wives, or relieve them entirely, if they lent a hand in this 'women's work'. But no, that would go against the 'privilege and dignity of the husband'. He demands that he have rest and comfort. The domestic life of the woman is a daily sacrifice of self to a thousand insignificant trifles. The ancient rights of her husband, her lord and master, survive unnoticed. Objectively, his slave takes her revenge. Also in concealed form. Her backwardness and her lack of understanding for her husband's revolutionary ideals act as a drag on his fighting spirit, on his determination to fight. They are like tiny worms, gnawing and undermining imperceptibly, slowly but surely. I know the life of the workers, and not only from books. Our communist work among the masses of women, and our political work in general, involves considerable educational work among the men. We must root out the old slave-owner's point of view, both in the Party and among the masses. That is one of our political tasks, a task just as urgently necessary as the formation of a staff composed of comrades, men and women, with thorough theoretical and practical training for Party work among working women."

To my question about present-day conditions in Soviet Russia, Lenin replied:

"The government of the proletarian dictatorship—jointly with the Communist Party and the trade unions of course—makes every effort to overcome the backward views of men and women and thus uproot the old, non-communist psychology. It goes without saying that men and women are absolutely equal before the law. A sincere desire to give effect to this equality is evident in all spheres. We are enlisting women to work in the economy, the administration, legislation and government. All courses and educational institutions are open to them, so that they can improve their professional and social training. We are organising community kitchens and public dining-rooms, laundries and repair shops, crèches, kindergartens, children's homes and educational institutions of every kind. In brief, we are quite in earnest about carrying out the requirements of our programme to shift the functions of house-keeping and education from the individual household to society. Woman is thus being relieved from her old domestic slavery and all dependence on her husband. She is enabled to give her capabilities and inclinations full play in society. Children are offered better opportunities for their development than at home. We have the most progressive female labour legislation in the world, and it is enforced by authorised representatives of organised labour. We are establishing maternity homes, mother-and-child homes, mothers' health centres, courses for infant and child care, exhibitions of mother and child care, and the like. We are making every effort to provide for needy and unemployed women.

"We know perfectly well that all this is still too little, considering the needs of the working women, and that it is still far from sufficient for their real emancipation. Yet it is an immense stride forward from what there was in tsarist and capitalist Russia. Moreover, it is a lot as compared with the state of affairs where capitalism still holds undivided sway. It is a good start in the right direction, and we shall continue to develop it consistently, and with all available energy, too. You abroad may rest assured. Because with each day that passes it becomes clearer that we cannot make progress without the millions of women. Think what this means in a country where the peasants comprise a solid 80% of the population. Small peasant farming implies individual housekeeping and the bondage of women. You will be far better off than we are in this respect, provided your proletarians at last grasp that the time is historically ripe for seizure of power, for revolution. In the meantime, we are not giving way to despair, des-pite the great difficulties. Our forces grow as the latter increase. Practical necessity will also impel us to find new ways of emancipating the masses of women. In combi-nation with the Soviet state, comradely solidarity will ac-complish wonders. To be sure, I mean comradely solidar-ity in the communist, not in the bourgeois, sense, in which it is preached by the reformists, whose revolutionary enthusiasm has evaporated like the smell of cheap vine-gar. Personal initiative, which grows into, and fuses with collective activity, should accompany comradely solidarity. Under the proletarian dictatorship the emancipation of women through the realisation of communism will proceed also in the countryside. In this respect I expect much from the electrification of our industry and agriculture. That is a grand scheme! The difficulties in its way are great, monstrously great. Powerful forces latent in the masses will have to be released and trained to overcome them. Millions of women must take part in this."

Someone had knocked twice in the last ten minutes, but Lenin had continued to speak. Now he opened the door and shouted:

"I'm coming!"

Turning in my direction, he added with a smile:

"You know, Clara, I am going to take advantage of the fact that I was conversing with a woman and will name the notorious female loquacity as the excuse for being late. Although this time it was the man and not the woman who did most of the talking. In general, I must say that you are really a good listener. But it was this that probably prompted me to talk so much."

With this jocular remark Lenin helped me on with my coat.

"You should dress more warmly," he suggested solicitously. "Moscow is not Stuttgart. You need someone to look after you. Don't catch cold. Good-bye."

He shook my hand firmly.

* * *

I had another talk with Lenin on the women's movement about a fortnight later. Lenin came to see me. As almost always, his visit was unexpected. It was an impromptu visit and occurred during an intermission in the gigantic burden of work accomplished by the leader of the victorious revolution. Lenin looked very tired and worried. Wrangel had not yet been crushed and the question of supplying the big cities with food confronted the Soviet Government like an inexorable sphinx.

Lenin asked how the theses were coming along. I told him that a big commission had been in session, which all prominent women Communists then in Moscow had attended and where they had spoken their opinions. The theses were ready and were now to be discussed by a small committee. Lenin pointed out that we should strive to have the Third World Congress[40] examine the problem with due thoroughness. This fact alone would break down the prejudice of many comrades. Anyhow, the women Communists should be the first to take things in hand, and with vigour.

"Don't twitter like a bunch of chatterboxes, but speak out loudly and clearly like fighters should," Lenin exclaimed with animation. "A congress is not a parlour where women display their charm, as we read in novels. A congress is a battlefield in which we fight for the knowledge we need for revolutionary action. Show that you can fight. In the first place, of course, against our enemies, but also within the Party, should the need arise. After all, the broad masses of women are at stake. Our Russian Party will back all proposals and measures that will help to win these masses. If the women are not with us, the counter-revolutionaries may succeed in setting them against us. We must always bear this in mind."

"We must win the mass of women over even if they are riveted to heaven by chains, as Stralsund puts it," I said, pursuing Lenin's idea. "Here, in the centre of the revolution with its richly seething life, with its strong, rapid pulse, a plan has occurred to me of a big, joint international action among the working women. It was prompted primarily by your big non-partisan women's conferences and congresses. We should try to transform them from national into international ones. It is a fact that the world war and its aftermath have deeply shaken the bulk of the women of various classes and sections of society. They are in ferment. They have been set in motion. Their distressing worries about securing a livelihood and the search for the purpose of life confront them with problems which most of them had hardly suspected and only a small minority had grasped in the past. Bourgeois society is unable to provide a satisfactory answer to their questions. Only communism can do it. We must rouse the broad masses of women in the capitalist countries to consciousness and should for that purpose call a non-partisan international women's congress."

Lenin did not reply at once. He sat lost in thought, considering the problem, his lips pursed, the lower lip protruding slightly.

"Yes, we ought to do it," he said finally. "The plan is good. But a good plan, even an excellent one, is worthless unless it is well executed. Have you thought about how it should be executed? What are your ideas on this score?"

I set out my ideas to Lenin in detail. To begin with, we ought to form a committee of Communist women from various countries in close and constant contact with our national sections. This committee would prepare, conduct and make use of the congress. It had to be decided whether it would be desirable for the committee to work openly and officially from the very beginning. At any rate, it would be the first task of the committee members to make contact with the leaders of the organised female workers in each country, the proletarian political women's movement, bourgeois women's organisations of every trend and description, and finally the prominent female physicians, teachers, writers, etc., and to form national non-partisan preparatory committees. An international committee would be formed from among the members of these national committees to prepare and convene the international congress, to draw up its agenda and to pick the time and place for the congress.

In my opinion the congress ought first to discuss the women's right to engage in trades and professions. In doing so it should deal with the questions of unemployment, equal pay for equal work, legislation on the 8-hour day and labour protection for women, organisation of trade unions, social care of mother and child, social measures to relieve housewives and mothers, etc. Furthermore, the agenda should deal with the status of women in marriage and family legislation and in public and political law. After substantiating these proposals I explained how the national committees in the various countries should thoroughly prepare the ground for the congress by a planned campaign at meetings and in the press. This campaign was particularly important in rousing the biggest possible number of women, to stimulate a serious study of the problems submitted for discussion, and to draw their attention to the congress and thereby to communism and the parties of the Communist International. The campaign had to reach the working women of all social strata. It would have to secure attendance and participation in the congress of representatives of all organisations concerned, and also of delegates from public women's meetings. The congress was to be a "popular representative body" entirely different from a bourgeois parliament.

It went without saying that women Communists were to be not merely the motive but also the leading force in the preparatory work, and should have the energetic support of our sections. Naturally, the same applied also to the work of the international committee, the work of the congress itself, and to its extensive use. Communist theses and resolutions on all items on the agenda should be submitted to the congress. They should be carefully worded and well reasoned with scholarly mastery of the relevant social facts. These theses should be discussed and approved beforehand by the Executive Committee of the Comintern. The communist solutions and slogans should be the focal point on which the work of the congress and public attention would concentrate. After the congress they should be disseminated among the broad masses of women by means of agitation and propaganda, so that they may become determinative for international women's mass actions. Needless to say, all this requires as an essential condition that women Communists work in all the committees and at the congress itself as a firm, solid body and that they act together on a lucid and unshakeable plan. There should be no out-of-turn actions.

In the course of my explanation Lenin nodded several times in approval and interposed a few remarks.

"It seems to me, dear comrade," he said, "that you have considered the matter very thoroughly in the political sense, and also the main points of the organisational angle. I fully agree that such a congress could accomplish much in the present situation. It offers us the opportunity of winning over the broad masses of women, particularly women in the various trades and professions, the industrial women workers and home-workers, the teachers and other professional women. This would be wonderful. Think of the situation in the big economic struggles or political strikes. What a reinforcement the revolutionary proletariat would gain in the class-conscious masses of women. Provided, of course, that we are able to win them over and keep them on our side. Our gain would be great. It would be nothing short of immense. But what would you say to the following few questions? The authorities will probably frown very severely upon the idea of this congress and will try to prevent it. However they are not likely to dare suppress it by brute force. Whatever they do will not frighten you. But are you not afraid that the women Communists will be overwhelmed in the committees and at the congress itself by the numerical superiority of the bourgeois and reformist delegates and their unquestionably greater experience? Besides, and most important, do you really have confidence in the Marxist schooling of our communist comrades, and are you sure that a shock group can be picked among them that will come out of the battle with honour?"

I told Lenin in reply that the authorities were not likely to use the mailed fist against the congress. Intrigues and boorish attacks against it would only act in its favour, and ours. We Communists could more than match the greater number and experience of the non-communist elements by the scientific superiority of historical materialism with its study and illumination of social problems, the perseverance with which we would demand that they be solved, and last but not least, by references to the victory of the proletarian revolution in Russia and its fundamental accomplishments in the work of emancipating the women. The weakness and lack of training of some of our comrades, their inexperience, could be compensated by planned preparation and teamwork. In this respect, I expect the very best from the Russian women comrades. They would form the iron core of our phalanx. In their company I would calmly brave much more hazardous clashes than the congress battles. Besides, even if we are outvoted, the very fact that we fought will put communism in the foreground and will have a big propaganda effect. Furthermore, it will give us points of departure for subsequent work.

Lenin laughed heartily.

"You are as enthusiastic as ever about the Russian women revolutionaries. Yes indeed, old love is not forgotten. I think you are right. Even defeat after a stubborn struggle would be a gain; it would prepare the ground for future gains among the working women. All things considered, it is a risk worth taking. It cannot possibly prove a total failure. But naturally, I hope for victory and wish you success from the bottom of my heart. It would considerably enhance our strength, it would widen and fortify our battlefront, it would put life into our ranks and set them in motion. That is always useful. Moreover, the congress would foment and increase unrest, uncertainty, contradictions and conflicts in the camp of the bourgeoisie and its reformist friends. One can just imagine who is going to sit down with the 'hyenas of the revolution', and, if things go well, to deliberate under their leadership. It will be the brave, well-disciplined female Social-Democrats under the supreme guidance of Scheidemann, Dittmann and Legien; the pious Christian women blessed by the Pope or devoted to Luther; daughters of privy counsellors, wives of newly-appointed councillors of state, lady-like English pacifists and ardent French suffragettes. What a picture of chaos, of the decay of the bourgeois world the congress is bound to present! What a portrayal of its hopeless conditions! The congress would add to the division and thereby weaken the forces of the counter-revolution. Every weakening of the enemy is tantamount to a strengthening of our forces. I am in favour of the congress. You will get our vigorous support. So get started, and I wish you luck in the struggle."

We spoke then about the situation in Germany, particularly the impending "Unity Congress" of the old Spartacists[41] and the Left wing of the Independents.[42] Thereupon, Lenin left in a hurry, exchanging friendly greetings with several comrades working in the room he had had to cross.

I set about the preparatory work with high hopes. However, the congress floundered, because it was opposed by the German and Bulgarian women comrades who were then leaders of the biggest communist women's movements outside Soviet Russia. They were flatly against calling the congress.

When I informed Lenin of this he answered:

"It is a pity, a great pity! These comrades missed a splendid opportunity to give a new and better outlook of hope for the masses of women and thereby to draw them into the revolutionary struggles of the proletariat. Who can tell whether such a favourable opportunity will recur in the near future? One should strike while the iron is hot. But the task remains. You must look for a way to reach the masses of women whom capitalism has plunged into dire need. You must look for it on all accounts. There is no evading this imperative task. Without the organised activity of the masses under communist leadership there can be no victory over capitalism and no building of communism. And so the hitherto dormant masses of women must be finally set into motion."

* * *

The first year spent by the revolutionary proletariat without Lenin has passed. It has shown the strength of his cause. It has proved the leader's great genius. It has shown how great and irreplaceable the loss has been. Salvoes mark the sad hour when Lenin closed his far-seeing, penetrating eyes for ever, a year ago. I see an endless procession of mourning working people, as they go to Lenin's resting-place. Their mourning is my mourning, the mourning of the millions. My newly-awakened grief evokes overwhelming memories in me of the reality that makes the painful present recede. I hear again every word Lenin spoke in conversation with me. I see every change in his face. . . . Banners are lowered at Lenin's tomb. They are banners steeped in the blood of fighters for the revolution. Laurel wreaths are laid. Not one of them is superfluous. And I add to them these modest lines.

Translated from the German

Notes

1 *Obukhov defence*—the heroic fight put up by the workers of the Obukhov plant in St. Petersburg against police and troops on May 7, 1901. Protests had been raised over the dismissal of 26 workers for participating in a May Day meeting, and on May 7, following the refusal of the management to reinstate the discharged men, 5,000 workers called a strike. Their demands included introduction of an eight-hour working day, a holiday on the 1st of May, reinstatement of the discharged men, and an increase in wages. Police and troops sent to disperse the strikers were met with a hail of stones. Only after strong reinforcements had been sent up were the police and the troops able to break up the demonstration.

The workers sustained some casualties, 800 workers were arrested and 29 of them were sent to penal servitude. The brutal reprisals meted out by the police evoked strikes of protest at a number of St. Petersburg works.

The Obukhov defence was of great importance in the history of the working-class movement in Russia. It marked the beginning of open political struggle by the working class.　　　　　　　　　　p. 6

2 The *Emancipation of Labour group*—the first Russian Marxist group, founded by G. V. Plekhanov in Geneva in 1883. Its members included P.B. Axelrod and V. I. Zasulich.

The group did much to spread Marxism in Russia. It published a "Library of Modern Socialism" series, which included translations of such works by Marx and Engels as "Manifesto of the Communist Party", "Wage Labour and Capital", "Socialism: Utopian and Scientific", as well as works by members of the group (G. V. Plekhanov's "Socialism and the Political Struggle", "Our Differences", etc.). The works by members of the group, particularly those of Plekhanov, criticised Narodnik views and discussed the basic questions of scientific socialism.

The group, however, committed some grave errors. They misconceived the role of the liberal bourgeoisie in the revolution and underestimated the revolutionary role of the peasants and the importance of the alliance between the proletariat and peasants for victory over tsarism.

In its work the Emancipation of Labour group was not connected with the mass working-class movement.

The group "merely laid a theoretical foundation for the Social-Democratic movement and took the first step towards the working-class movement" (Lenin). p. 7

3 The *International Socialist Congress in Stuttgart* (the Seventh Congress of the Second International) was held on August 18-24, 1907.

The R.S.D.L.P. sent 37 delegates to the Congress. The Bolsheviks were represented by Lenin, Litvinov, Lunacharsky and others. The Congress discussed the following questions: 1) militarism and international conflicts; 2) relations between political parties and trade unions; 3) the colonial question; 4) immigration and emigration of workers and 5) women's franchise. The Congress was the scene of a clash between the revolutionary wing of the international socialist movement, represented by the Russian Bolsheviks with Lenin at their head, the German Left Social-Democrats Rosa Luxemburg and others, and the opportunist wing (Vollmar, Bernstein and others). The opportunists suffered a defeat—and the Congress adopted resolutions which supplied a revolutionary Marxist formulation of the main tasks of the socialist parties. p. 7

4 *Cadets*—members of the Constitutional-Democratic Party—the leading party of the liberal monarchist bourgeoisie in Russia. It was formed in October 1905 and included representatives of the bourgeoisie, Zemstvo leaders from among the landowners, and bourgeois intellectuals. Subsequently it became a party of the imperialist bourgeoisie.

During the First World War the Constitutional-Democrats gave their wholehearted support to the tsarist government so as to help the Russian imperialist bourgeoisie achieve its predatory aims. In 1917, when the party was represented in the bourgeois Provisional Government, it instigated anti-revolutionary struggle.

After the victory of the October Socialist Revolution the Constitutional-Democrats became irreconcilable enemies of Soviet power and took part in all counter-revolutionary actions and the campaigns of the interventionists. p. 9

5 *Women Delegates' Conferences* were set up at factories, in villages and workers' settlements. Broad sections of women factory workers and peasants elected delegates to these bodies. Women delegates were attached to various Soviet, co-operative and trade union organisations (departments of Soviets, various commissions) for the purpose of organising and supervising the work of educational and medical institutions, nurseries, children's playgrounds, canteens, shops, etc.

In the period from the establishment of Soviet power up to 1933 the Delegates' Conferences were the main form of the Communist Party's work among women. The conferences played an important role in developing women's political consciousness and in drawing them into state administration and the country's social life.

The Delegates' Conferences functioned under the guidance of the corresponding primary Party organisations, which appointed women organisers for work among women and for guiding the activities of the Delegates' Conferences.

A great number of women who were subsequently appointed to leading Party, Soviet and managerial posts had passed through the school of the Delegates' Conferences.   p. 10

6 *Kulaks*—"rich peasants who exploit other people's labour either by hiring workers or by lending money on interest, etc." (Lenin). p. 11

7 *Political departments* were set up by the Central Committee of the Communist Party for the purpose of enhancing leadership and strengthening political work on those fronts of socialist construction which were of particular importance for the national economy and the country.

The political departments at the MTSs were established in 1933 and existed till 1934.   p. 12

8 The *Party Programme* adopted at the Second Congress of the R.S.D.L.P. in 1903 was worked out by the editors of the Leninist *Iskra* between 1901 and 1902. The original drafts of the programme had been made by Plekhanov. Realising that Plekhanov's drafts were not acceptable, Lenin worked out a draft of his own in January-February 1902. The *Iskra* editorial board appointed a commission to draw up a single draft programme based on the drafts made by Lenin and Plekhanov. Lenin insisted on inserting in the final draft the extremely important clause on the dictatorship of the proletariat, a clear-cut definition of the proletariat's leading role in the revolution, and on laying a special emphasis on the proletarian character of the Party. Lenin also drew up the agrarian part of the programme. The draft programme was published in *Iskra* No. 21 on June 1, 1902.   p. 17

9 *Factory Courts* were supposed to deal with conflicts between workers and employers concerning wages, labour protection, etc., and pass decisions on them. Agricultural courts were to be vested with the right to lower very high rents, invalidate shackling contracts, etc.   p. 19

10 *Fabian society*—a reformist society founded in 1884 by a group of bourgeois intellectuals in Britain. It was called after the Roman general Fabius Cunctator (the "delayer") known for his cautious tactics and avoidance of decisive battles. The Fabians renounced the class struggle and set themselves the task of "permeating" the bourgeoisie with "socialist" ideas. They maintained that it was possible to effect transition to socialism by means of petty reforms. In 1900 the Fabian society joined the Labour Party.   p. 20

11 *Malthusianism*—reactionary doctrine propounded by the English economist Thomas Malthus (1766-1834), who sought to prove that the population was growing faster than the means of subsistence and that the misery and poverty of the working class under capitalism were due to the rapid growth of the population, and not to the capitalist exploitation of the workers.

Malthusianism was an attempt on the part of bourgeois ideologists to exonerate capitalism and to prove the inevitability of privation and misery for the working class under any social system. It was an attempt to conceal from the masses the real causes of their grievous conditions and to divert them from the struggle against the capitalist system.

Marx scathingly criticised the theory of Malthus and proved that the poverty of the masses was the product of capitalism and that it was caused by the appropriation of the workers' unpaid labour by the capitalists. He showed that the destruction of capitalism and transition to socialism would put an end to the misery and privations of the working class.

Marx showed that no overall law of the growth of population actually existed and that every socio-economic formation had its own law of population growth.

In the 1870s Malthusianism reappeared in the shape of neo-malthusianism which tried to justify the growing impoverishment of the working people by pseudo-scientific theories of "absolute overpopulation", diminishing returns of the soil, etc. Neomalthusianism regards birth control, wars and epidemics as means of bolstering up capitalism and alleviating the misery of the masses. Many of its exponents advocate race discrimination.   p. 28

[12] *Pirogov Congresses*—congresses of Russian doctors convened by the Russian Doctors' Society in memory of the great Russian surgeon and anatomist N. I. Pirogov.

In this article the reference is to the XII Pirogov Congress held in St. Petersburg on May 29-June 5, 1913.   p. 28

[13] *Russkoye Slovo (Russian Word)*—a liberal-bourgeois newspaper which appeared in Moscow from 1885 to 1917.   p. 28

[14] *Leipziger Volkszeitung*—German Social-Democratic daily newspaper published from 1894 to 1933.   p. 31

[15] *Narodniks*—representatives of an ideological and political trend which arose in Russia in the 1870s.

The distinctive features of the Narodnik ideology were the denial of the leading role of the proletariat in the revolutionary movement and the erroneous belief that socialist revolution could be carried out by the small proprietors, the peasants. They regarded the village commune, which was actually a relic of feudalism and serfdom in the Russian countryside, as a nucleus of socialism, etc. Narodnik socialism was divorced from the actual development of society and was merely a phrase, a dream, a pious wish.

In the 1880s and 1890s the Narodniks reconciled themselves to tsarism, began to champion the interests of the kulaks and fought furiously against Marxism.   p. 33

[16] This refers to a pamphlet which Inessa Armand intended to write for working women, but never did.   p. 36

[17] *Organising Committee* (O.C.)—the leading centre of the Mensheviks, formed in 1912.   p. 44

[18] *Golos (Voice)*—Menshevik and Trotskyist daily newspaper; it appeared in Paris from September 1914 to January 1915.   p. 44

[19] These theses were written in Russian and German, translated into French by Inessa Armand and distributed among Swiss Left-wing Social-Democrats for discussion.

The *Zimmerwald Left group* was formed by Lenin at the First Socialist Conference of the Internationalists, held at the beginning of September 1915 in Zimmerwald (Switzerland). Lenin described the conference as "a first step" in the development of the international anti-war movement. In the Zimmerwald Left group only the Bolsheviks led by Lenin occupied the correct, thoroughly consistent anti-war position.   p. 45

[20] The present publication contains an extract from the draft R.S.D.L.P. programme drawn up in April-May 1917. For convenience of reading Lenin put together the old and the new text of the programme; those parts of the old programme that remained unchanged in the new programme are given in *ordinary type* and those which are to be completely deleted are given in *italics*. Those parts of the new programme that were in the old programme are given in bold type.
                                                                                p. 48

[21] *Mensheviks*—adherents of a petty-bourgeois opportunist trend in the Russian Social-Democratic movement who spread bourgeois influence among the working class. They came to be called Mensheviks after the Second Congress of the R.S.D.L.P. in August 1903, when they were in the minority ("menshinstvo" in Russian) during the election of the central Party bodies, while the revolutionary Social-Democrats headed by Lenin received a majority ("bolshinstvo" in Russian) and were called Bolsheviks. The Mensheviks sought to bring about an agreement between the proletariat and the bourgeoisie and pursued an opportunist line in the working-class movement. After the February 1917 revolution the Mensheviks along with the Socialist-Revolutionaries entered the bourgeois Provisional Government, supported its imperialist policy and fought against the growing proletarian revolution.

After the October Socialist Revolution the Menshevik Party became openly counter-revolutionary, and organised and took part in conspiracies and revolts aimed at the overthrow of Soviet power.

Socialist-Revolutionaries—a petty-bourgeois party founded at the end of 1901 and the beginning of 1902. At first the party expressed the democratic demands of the peasants and their desire to take over the landed estates. As time went on, however, it became the party of the kulaks and, following the October Socialist Revolution, an openly counter-revolutionary party which joined forces with the bourgeoisie, the landowners and foreign interventionists in their struggle against Soviet power. The S.R.s called themselves socialists, but their socialism was a far cry from scientific socialism, from Marxism. It was a petty-bourgeois equalitarian socialism based on the so-called "socialisation of the land" and equalitarian use of the land according to labour standards, which actually meant the provision of the most favourable conditions for the development of capitalism.   p. 57

[22] *The First All-Russia Congress of Working Women* was convened by the Central Committee of the R.C.P.(B.) in Moscow, November 16-21, 1918. It was attended by 1,147 women delegates from factories and the rural poor. The Congress approved the foreign policy of the Soviet Government and called upon women workers and peasants to support and champion it. The Congress approved

the establishment of delegates' conferences as a new organisational form of drawing non-Party working women into socialist construction. The Congress marked the beginning of extensive Party work among women workers and peasants.   p. 59

[23] *Poor Peasant Committees* were set up by decree of the All-Russia Central Executive Committee on June 11, 1918. The following questions fell within the competence of the committees: distribution of grain, necessaries of life and implements, assistance to local food organs in requisitioning grain surpluses held by kulaks and rich peasants. The decree granted privileges to the poor peasants with regard to the distribution of grain and agricultural implements.

The Poor Peasant Committees were the strongholds of the dictatorship of the proletariat in the countryside. They played an important part in the struggle against the kulaks, in re-distributing confiscated lands and supplying food for the industrial centres and the Red Army. The setting up of these committees was a further step in the development of socialist revolution in the countryside, where they contributed to the consolidation of Soviet power and were of tremendous importance in winning the middle peasants over to the side of Soviet power.

By decision of the Extraordinary Sixth Congress of Soviets (November 1918) the Poor Peasant Committees, which had by that time fulfilled their tasks were merged with the village Soviets. p. 60

[24] Materials and documents written by Lenin for a draft programme of the R.C.P.(B.) formed the basis of the work of the commission which drafted the Party Programme. A new Party Programme was adopted at the Eighth Congress of the R.C.P.(B.) in March 1919. p. 62

[25] *Communist subbotniks*—voluntary unpaid work indicative of the working people's communist attitude towards labour.

The first subbotniks were organised during the Civil War, when the economy was ruined and there was a shortage of labour. In response to the letter of the R.C.P. Central Committee calling upon them to work in *a revolutionary way* the workers of the Moscow-Kazan railway line turned out for the first communist subbotnik on Saturday, May 10, 1919. After knocking-off time they put in 6 hours' extra work repairing railway carriages and locomotives, loading materials and performing other jobs without payment. Their initiative evoked a response and subbotniks became a mass movement.

On May 1, 1920, an all-Russia subbotnik was organised.

Communist subbotniks played an important part in the period of the economic rehabilitation and development after the Civil War and foreign military intervention. They aroused a mighty wave of socialist emulation. Lenin attached great importance to communist subbotniks and called them a "great beginning" in "the development of labour productivity, in the establishment of a new labour discipline and the creation of the socialist conditions of economy and life".   p. 63

[26] *Pood*—an old Russian measure of weight equal to 16.381 kg. p. 65

[27] The *Constituent Assembly* was convened by the Soviet Government on January 5, 1918. Elections to the Constituent Assembly had in the main been held before the October Socialist Revolution, and its

composition reflected the past stage in the country's development, when state power was in the hands of the Mensheviks, Socialist-Revolutionaries and Constitutional-Democrats. There was a wide gap between the will of the vast majority of the people, which found expression in the establishment of Soviet power and its decrees, and the policy conducted by the Socialist-Revolutionary, Menshevik and Constitutional-Democrat section of the Constituent Assembly, which championed the interests of the bourgeoisie and the kulaks. The Assembly refused to discuss "The Declaration of the Rights of the Working and Exploited People" proposed by the Bolsheviks and to approve the decrees on peace and the land, and the decree transferring state power to the Soviets, which were adopted by the Second Congress of Soviets.

After making their declaration, the Bolsheviks walked out of the Constituent Assembly which had only to clearly revealed its hostility towards the genuine interests of the working people. On January 7, 1918, the Constituent Assembly was dissolved by decree of the All-Russia Central Executive Committee.   p. 68

[28] *International Working Women's Day* or International Women's Day, March 8, is a day of international unity of working women all over the world in the struggle for peace, democracy and socialism.

March 8 was instituted as the International Women's Day on the proposal of Clara Zetkin at the Second International Conference of Women Socialists, held at Copenhagen in 1910, with the aim of mobilising broad sections of women for the struggle against bourgeois domination. International Women's Day was first observed in 1911 in Germany, Austria, Denmark and Switzerland. It was first observed in Russia in 1913.   p. 80

[29] *Communist International* (Comintern, the Third International)— international revolutionary organisation of the proletariat, which existed from 1919 to 1943. It was a union of communist parties of different countries.

The Comintern set itself the task of winning the working people for the cause of communism, achieving dictatorship of the proletariat, abolishing the capitalist system and replacing it with the socialist system, and doing away with the exploitation of man by man. The Comintern restored and cemented the ties between the working people of all countries which had been disrupted as a result of the treachery of the Second International leaders during the First World War; it upheld the doctrine of Marxism-Leninism and prevented its being distorted by the opportunists; it worked out a number of theoretical problems of the working-class movement and the struggle for socialism between the two world wars, did much to spread the ideas of scientific socialism among the masses and helped to strengthen the communist parties of various countries.

It was dissolved in May 1943 by a decision of the Executive Committee of the Comintern, because under the new conditions the former organisational form of leadership of the working-class movement fell short of the requirements of the day.   p. 81

[30] The *First Conference of Representatives of Women's Departments of the Peoples of Soviet Regions and Republics in the East* was held

in Moscow on April 5-7, 1921. It was attended by 45 women communist delegates from Turkestan, Azerbaijan, Bashkiria, the Crimea, the Caucasus, the Tatar Republic, Siberia and a number of gubernias with Turkic and mountain population. The Conference delegates addressed a letter to Lenin inviting him to attend the conference. The telephone message published here was Lenin's reply to the invitation. p. 86

[31] *Pod Znamenem Marxizma (Under the Banner of Marxism)*—a monthly philosophical, social and economic magazine, which appeared in Moscow from January 1922 till June 1944. p. 90

[32] *Ekonomist*—a journal published by the Industrial-Economic Department of the Russian Technical Society in Petrograd, 1921-22. p. 90

[33] *Non-Party Conference of Factory and Peasant Women of Moscow City and Moscow Gubernia* met on November 6, 1922. There were more than 2,000 delegates. Lenin's message of greetings was given to the delegates who went to invite him to speak at the conference. p. 93

[34] The *Second Congress of the Communist International* met between July 19 and August 7, 1920. p. 97

[35] *Military Cadets*—in tsarist Russia those attending officer schools. During the Great October Socialist Revolution and in the period that immediately followed they offered armed resistance to the insurgent people and Soviet power in Petrograd, Moscow and some other towns but were everywhere defeated. p. 98

[36] *The Treaty of Versailles*—imperialist peace treaty which concluded the First World War. It was signed in Versailles on June 28, 1919 by the U.S.A., Great Britain, France, Italy, Japan and other countries, on the one hand, and defeated Germany, on the other.

The Versailles Treaty was designed to consolidate the redivision of the capitalist world in favour of the victor powers. France obtained Alsace-Lorraine, the Saar region was put under the administration of the League of Nations for 15 years and the collieries in this region became French property. The German colonies were divided among the victor countries. Germany had to pay an enormous sum of reparations.

The whole burden imposed by the Treaty of Versailles was borne by the German people, who had to pay huge taxes and suffer the ordeal of chronic unemployment. As for the imperialist industrial tycoons, they retained their dominant positions in the country and continued to pocket huge profits. p. 103

[37] The reference is to the war launched by the bourgeois-landowning Poland against the Soviet Republic in April 1920. p. 109

[38] *Communist Workers' Party of Germany*—anarchist-syndicalist petty-bourgeois group, formed in 1919 by the "Left" elements which had split from the Communist Party of Germany. Lacking support among the German workers, the group degenerated into an insignificant sect hostile to the Communist Party and the working class. p. 111

³⁹ *The Second International*—an international union of socialist parties founded in 1889. When the First World War broke out, the leaders of the Second International betrayed socialism and went over to the side of their imperialist governments. Thus the Second International collapsed. The Left groups and parties affiliated with the Second International joined the Communist (Third) International founded in Moscow in 1919. The Second International was resurrected at a conference in Berne (Switzerland) in the same year 1919. Only the parties which represented the Right, opportunist wing of the socialist movement joined it.   p. 112

⁴⁰ The *Third Congress of the Comintern* held on June 22-July 12, 1921, heard a report by Clara Zetkin on the revolutionary women's movement and adopted the following resolutions: 1) On strengthening international ties of women communists and the tasks of the International Secretariat of the Comintern with regard to work among women and 2) On the forms and methods of communist work among women.   p. 117

⁴¹ The *Spartacists*—members of the Spartacus League, a revolutionary organisation of the German Left Social-Democrats founded at the beginning of the First World War by Karl Liebknecht, Rosa Luxemburg, Franz Mehring, Clara Zetkin, Jogiches (Tyszka) and others. Members of the Spartacus League carried on revolutionary propaganda among the masses against the imperialist war and exposed the predatory policy of the German imperialists and the treachery of Social-Democratic leaders. On a number of theoretical and tactical questions, however, they held erroneous views. Lenin criticised their mistakes in "The Junius Pamphlet", "The Caricature of Marxism and 'Imperialist Economism'", and other works. In April 1917 the Spartacus League affiliated with the Centrist Independent Social-Democratic Party of Germany retaining its organisational independence. After the November 1918 revolution in Germany the Spartacus League broke with the "Independents" and founded the Communist Party of Germany in December 1918. p. 122

⁴² The *Independent Social-Democratic Party of Germany*—Centrist party formed in April 1917 from the opposition groups within the German Social-Democratic Party.

In October 1920 the party split at its congress in Halle. The greater part united with the Communist Party of Germany in December 1920, the Right-wing elements forming a separate party and adopting the old name of the Independent Social-Democratic Party. In 1922 the "Independents" re-joined the German Social-Democratic Party.   p. 122

Name Index

A

Adler, Viktor (1852-1918)—one of the founders of the Austrian Social-Democratic Party; afterwards a reformist leader of the Second International.—20, 21

d'Annunzio, Gabriele (1863-1938) —decadent Italian writer and politician, chauvinist during the First World War. —107

Armand, Inessa (Yelizaveta Fyodorovna) (1875-1920)— prominent figure in the international women's and communist movement; joined the R.S.D.L.P. in 1904.—36, 38, 109

Astrakhan, I. D. (1862-1918)— doctor, author of a number of works on social insurance, prevention of accidents, etc. —28, 29

B

Bebel, August (1840-1913)— prominent leader of the German and international working-class movement, one of the founders and leaders of German Social-Democracy. By profession a turner.—101

Breshko-Breshkovskaya, Yekaterina Konstantinovna (1844-1934)—one of the organisers and leaders of the Party of Socialist-Revolutionaries, belonged to the extreme Right wing; after the October Socialist Revolution of 1917 she came out against Soviet Government.—9, 55, 58

C

Chernov, Viktor Mikhailovich (1876-1952)—leader of the Socialist-Revolutionary Party; Minister for Agriculture in the bourgeois Provisional Government; one of the organisers of the counter-revolutionary actions against Soviet government after the October Socialist Revolution of 1917; counter-revolutionary émigré after 1920.—58

D

Denikin, Anton Ivanovich (1872-1947)—general of the tsarist army, one of the leaders of the counter-revolution organised by the bourgeoisie and the landowners. In 1919 he headed the whiteguard armies of the south of Russia during their drive towards Moscow. In March 1920 his forces were routed by the Red Army; Denikin fled abroad.—68

Dittmann, Wilhelm (1874-1954)
—one of the leaders of German Social-Democrats, Centrist.—122

E

Engels, Frederick (1820-1895).—57, 106

F

Freud, Sigmund (1856-1939)—Austrian neuropathologist and psychologist; he regarded human behaviour as being based on sex instinct.—101
Frey—see *Lenin, V. I.*

G

Gärtner—official of the Austrian Ministry of Railways, member of the International Society for Combating Prostitution.—31
Gorbunova (Kablukova), M. K. (1840-1931)—economist and statistician, writer of Narodnik trend.—14

J

Jogiches, Leon (Tyszka) (1867-1919)—prominent figure in the Polish and German working-class movement; together with Rosa Luxemburg fought against Centrists among German Social-Democrats.—99

K

Key, Ellen (1849-1926)—Swedish bourgeois writer, author of works on women's movement and education of children.—40
Kharizomenov, S. A. (1854-1917) —Russian Zemstvo statistician and economist.—14, 16
Kolchak, Alexander Vasilyevich (1873-1920)—Admiral; in 1918, with the help of the U.S., Brittish and French imperialists, established military dictatorship of the bourgeoisie and the landowners in the Urals, Siberia and Far East. In the spring of 1920 he headed the offensive against the Soviet Republic. By February 1920 his forces had been routed by the Red Army.—68
Krupskaya, Nadezhda Konstantinovna (1869-1939)—prominent Soviet woman statesman, one of the oldest members of the C.P.S.U., wife and close associate of Lenin, outstanding Soviet educationalist.—12

L

Legien, Carl (1861-1920)—German Right-wing Social-Democrat, a trade union leader; revisionist; extreme social-chauvinist during the First World War.—122
Lenin, Vladimir Ilyich (1870-1924).—5-9, 10, 11, 12, 18, 19, 93, 95-123
Lichkus, L. G. (1858-1926)—doctor, director of the Mariinsky Maternity Home in St. Petersburg.—28
Luther, Martin (1483-1546)—German religious reformer, theologian, and publicist.—122
Luxemburg, Rosa (1871-1919)—prominent figure in the international working-class movement and the Left wing of the Second International, one of the founders of the German Communist Party.—42, 99, 100

M

Marx, Karl (1818-1883).—10
Morgans—family of American multi-millionaires.—25
Morley, John (1838-1923)—Eng-

lish politician and writer, Liberal, Secretary of State for India from 1905 to 1910, suppressed national liberation movement.—23

Morozovs—big textile manufacturers in Russia.—25

P

Plekhanov, G. V. (1856-1918)—prominent leader of the Russian and international socialist movement; outstanding propagandist of Marxism; afterwards a Menshevik.—58

Popp, Adelheid (b. 1869)—Austrian Social-Democrat, publicist and writer, founder and leader of the women's Social-Democratic movement in Austria.—20

R

Ramsay, William (1852-1916)—English chemist, known mainly for his works in the field of physical chemistry.—24, 25

Rockefellers—family of American multi-millionaires.—25

Rothstein, F. A. (1871-1953)—Russian Social-Democrat; compelled to emigrate from Russia in 1890, he became active in the British Labour movement and was one of the founders of the Communist Party of Great Britain (1920). Author of a number of works on the history of imperialism.—22

Ryabushinskys—big Russian capitalists and bankers.—25

S

Scheidemann, Philipp (1865-1939)—one of the leaders of the extreme Right wing of German Social-Democracy;

head of the German bourgeois government in February-June 1919, one of the organisers of the brutal suppression of the German working-class movement between 1918 and 1921.—122

Sorokin, P. A. (b. 1889)—Socialist-Revolutionary. Before 1917 assistant-professor of the Petrograd University; between 1919-1922 professor of sociology at the Higher School in Petrograd; subsequently was expelled from Russia for counter-revolutionary activities.—90, 91

T

Tsereteli, I. G. (1882-1959)—one of the leaders of the Mensheviks, Minister of Posts and Telegraphs and later Minister of the Interior in the bourgeois Provisional Government (1917); head of the counter-revolutionary Menshevik Government in Georgia after the October Socialist Revolution of 1917; counter-revolutionary émigré after the triumph of Soviet power in Georgia in 1921.—9, 55, 58

V

Vigdorchik, N. A. (1874-1954)—doctor, author of a number of works on social insurance and occupational diseases.—28

W

Wrangel, P. N. (1878-1928)—general of the tsarist army, one of the leaders of counter-revolution in Russia during the Civil War. In April 1920 he became commander-in-chief of the counter-revolutionary "armed forces of the south of Russia". In November 1920, following the rout of his forces by the Red Army, he fled abroad.— 109, 117

Z

Zetkin, Clara (1857-1933)—prominent figure in the German and international working-class movement, one of the founders of the German Communist Party; organiser and leader of the international women's communist movement for many years.— 20, 21, 95-123

Zietz, Luise (1865-1922)—one of the leaders of the German Social-Democratic Party, teacher by profession; at the Stuttgart Congress of the Second International (1907) supported the demand for women's suffrage.—21